POLITICAL WOMAN

POLITICAL WOMAN – A MEMOIR

NUALA FENNELL

CURRACH
PRESS

First published in 2009 by

CURRACH PRESS

55A Spruce Avenue, Stillorgan Industrial Park, Blackrock, County Dublin

www.currach.ie

1 3 5 4 2

Cover by bluett

Origination by Currach Press

Printed in Ireland by ColourBooks, Baldoyle Industrial Estate, Dublin 13

ISBN: 978-1-85607-988-4

The author has asserted her moral rights.

CONTENTS

FOREWORD BY MAIREAD MCGUINNESS MEP

Every so often we are reminded of 'the good old days'.
And every so often we are reminded of the bad old days.
Nuala Fennell's memoir combines a bit of both, as seen
through the eyes of someone who knew from an early
age that the place and role of women in Irish society were
not to her liking. Or perhaps, more directly, that Irish
society was not to her liking.

Even as a young girl in the 1940s she saw in her mother
a yearning for something which, as the wife of a Garda
and the mother of several young children, she could not
have. In these formative years Nuala knew she wanted
something different for herself and for other women.

I did most of my growing up during the time when
Nuala Fennell was making her presence felt in the Ireland
of the late 1960s onwards. I have vague memories of that
Ireland but this book reminds me all too clearly that Irish
society was neither equal nor fair and that much needed
to be done to solve the problem. It was a time of opening
up, of awakening, of campaigning, of some success and
some failure too. Social change is never easy. And the job
is not entirely done.

Nuala Fennell, along with other like-minded women,
began a crusade to make a difference. They were viewed

with suspicion, yet they and others who joined them did make a real difference to many lives, including those who were secretly afraid of the changes they were attempting to bring about.

I can recall those heady days of the contraceptive train, the appearances of campaigning women on *The Late Late Show* and the gradually-awakening realisation among women themselves that they were treated less than fairly within Irish society. I remember that particular time as one of great debate nationally and within families. The McGuinness household of five daughters and three sons was a hotbed of such discussion. It seems embarrassing to admit that we would wait for the end of *The Late Late Show* before going out on a Saturday night; such was the intensity of the debate and the desire to catch every last word, in anticipation of the Sunday lunch discussion. How times have changed!

Nuala found herself, like many women, a wife and a mother of young children, yet desperately longing for something more and something different. In 1970 to start a crusade questioning the role of men and women in Irish society was, as she describes it, a tall order. But out of this desire was born the Irish Women's Liberation Movement, with colourful characters like Mary Kenny, Nell McCafferty, June Levine and Máirín de Búrca among its early campaigners.

Access to media was a key part of the progress made by the campaign and its ultimate success. It is interesting that Nuala Fennell turned to journalism to kick-start her work. The pen is mightier than the sword.

It is true that the Irish Women's Liberation Movement

did not last very long and indeed many saw its members as attention-seeking and irrelevant to the lives of 'ordinary' Irish women. Yet that campaign did have an impact and was the impetus for the establishment of other groups like AIM, Adapt, Irish Women's Aid, Cherish and FLAC. These groups dealt with the hidden Ireland: with the women and children who were living in fear in family homes with nowhere to turn to when things got tough. For many women, these organisations offered vital support and gave them the strength to get out of difficult situations. For others the relief was only temporary and some returned to difficult family situations. This story is as relevant today as it was thirty years ago and the important work of protecting women and children in violent situations continues. And, indeed, men in violent situations must also be protected.

It is worth noting that Nuala admits that Irish Women's Aid broke every rule in the planning and fire safety rule book in order to do what they had to do!

Until I read this book I did not realise, or perhaps I had forgotten, that there was a time when the domicile of a woman was that of her husband, so it was possible in the pre-divorce era for a woman to be divorced by her husband in another country without her choosing or even knowing.

The Irish Women's Liberation Movement politicised Nuala Fennell and strengthened her determination to make a difference. In 1977 she stood in the general election as an independent candidate. She recalls the naiveté among women, working with inadequate experience and not fully appreciating the fierce competition for nominations, the extensive male networks and the vested interests.

Nuala recalls the heady days of the early 1980s, Garret FitzGerald's charisma and women being drawn towards Fine Gael and towards politics.

Nuala won a seat in Dáil Éireann in 1981. Her recollection of the famous budget day of 1982 has a particular resonance for me. I was a young researcher on RTÉ's agriculture programme *Landmark* and we were preparing to go live on air with a post-budget programme when a call came through to the office from Ray MacSharry telling us that the government had fallen. All hell broke loose in the studio and in the country!

In 1982 Nuala's third election in eighteen months brought success again and a new job as Minister of State for Women's Affairs. Her interaction with some of the leading figures in the Catholic Church makes for fascinating reading. The questions of divorce and abortion loomed large and public debates were deeply divisive and bitter.

Nuala Fennell ran in the 1979 European election campaign – the first direct elections to the European Parliament. She recalls that canvassing for the EEC, as it was back then, was pushing an open door as far as most Irish women were concerned. The role of women at work had systematically improved since Ireland's entry to the EEC in 1973. Equal pay directives and other such initiatives were, as she says, 'the big sticks that forced successive Irish governments to prioritise women's rights'. It is worth noting that women seem less enthusiastic about the EU today than they were in the 1970s: the past may have been forgotten too readily.

Nuala's work in politics did make a difference but perhaps a younger generation of men and women do not know enough of the Ireland out of which we have emerged. They need to read this book to appreciate what Irish society was like and the significant changes that have come about.

Politics is not an easy profession, as Nuala was to discover. She describes rather brilliantly why so many people are needed to make an election campaign a success. Her reliance on the quiet support of her husband Brian is something I can personally vouch for in my own family situation. Every politician needs strong backup on the home scene. The campaign was about women but it also clearly needed and had the involvement of men.

So what of Ireland in 2009? On the face of it the equality war has been won but the battle remains to be fought. Women are still few in number in Irish political life. Does it have to be that way? Irish society has undoubtedly changed but the lives of many women remain difficult.

This book is a wake-up call to highlight where we were and the major changes that have taken place over a long period of time, as seen through the eyes of one female politician who was there at the start.

Without women like Nuala Fennell and her family, which supported her through thick and thin, these changes might have been slower in coming.

Preface

Like other memoir-writers, I had a few false starts over the years getting to grips with a book. One starts with very high expectations of the biography that might emerge: historically accurate, factually true and fair, standing up to forensic examination.

Well, this is the result, an honest account of my involvement in lobby campaign groups for women and the step-by-step advances I took into politics and as a minister of state in government.

If my granddaughters Eveline, Kate and Amelie, ask me in years to come why I wrote this book, I will tell them that I did so to ensure that any future analysis or scrutiny of women's activities from 1960s to 1980s would not second-guess what I did, said, or felt. In other words, I wrote it to set the record straight – and to show them what a good and fortunate time they are growing up in.

A lot of people encouraged me, nobody more so than Mary Kenny, my colleague in the trenches. She did not say, 'Please, continue with the writing.' She said, 'Nuala you just have to do it. You owe it.' No choice there. And Brian, my dearest life partner, beat the same kind of drum. So I had no means of escape.

I could never thank Brian enough for his love and

generosity throughout my life. He was at my elbow, provided ideas and insights, helped me when I got into scrapes, cooked wonderful meals and was a fun daddy, a stunning mother substitute to our three children. Every woman deputy should have a Brian!

My deepest gratitude to all my friends in AIM and Irish Women's Aid. They are the most unselfish and dedicated group of women and worked for years for a common cause, women's rights, in the best tradition of volunteerism. They brought about a considerable number of new laws and practices for Irish women.

I salute the pioneers in Women's Liberation who, after all, were in the vanguard of a changed Ireland.

Central to my sources was a journal I started in April 1974. At the beginning I intended it to record the children's early years but inevitably it reflected political events. Of inestimable help were Ted Nealon's guides to the Dáil and Seanad and the Institute of Public Administration diaries. Don't blame them for any inaccuracies: these are mine! I reread some of my feminist library and found all the milestones of the journey of Irish women up to that point in Mavis Arnold's 1987 book, *Irish Women into Focus*. Sean McCann's advice was not to read other political memoirs, which I didn't. But a peek was necessary now and then, to fill a gap or clarify a point.

Grateful appreciation to Jo O'Donoghue and Currach Press, who set me on the writing road, and especially to Mairead McGuinness MEP for her insightful foreword.

1

GOODBYE MR HAUGHEY

The members' restaurant in Leinster House on 4 November 1992 had the highly charged air that I knew from other pre-general-election days during my eleven years in Leinster House. The drama of unravelling the 26th Dáil was being enacted down in the chamber. Under the guise of a no-confidence debate, the pieces were being put in place for an exodus to the country as party leaders debated the reasons for the earlier than necessary election, all justifying their actions for the previous three years. Already deputies were drifting off to their constituencies, arms laden with boxes of envelopes and printed flyers.

At Pádraig Flynn's table nearby there was the sort of jollity and cheer more characteristic of the start of a new Dáil than its ending. Other Fianna Fáil deputies and senators joined the Flynn table, all in a high celebratory mood, toasting him and the other ministers who had just been given extra portfolios due to the resignations from the coalition government of Progressive Democrat cabinet ministers Bobby Molloy and Desmond O'Malley. With the minority PDs out of government, there was to be, for however short a while, a single-party Fianna Fáil administration. And that for Fianna Fáilers was a cause for celebration.

At its inception the 26th Dáil, elected on 15 June 1989, made history with Fianna Fáil conceding a 'core value' for the first time by forming a coalition government with the Progressive Democrats. Erstwhile opponents Desmond O'Malley, leader of the smaller party, and Charles Haughey, the outgoing Taoiseach and leader of Fianna Fáil, buried their differences and went into government together in July 1989. But in February 1992 Charles Haughey was implicated in the tapping of the phones of two prominent political journalists, Bruce Arnold and Geraldine Kennedy, when he was Taoiseach in 1982. Ten years earlier he had denied involvement, claiming it was solely the action of his then Minister for Justice, the late Sean Doherty. But quite unexpectedly Sean Doherty, who was a senator in 1992, told the truth, divulged Charles Haughey's role in the affair and forced his resignation as Taoiseach. Albert Reynolds, then Minister for Finance and an ardent anti-coalitionist, became leader of the party and Taoiseach.

It was only a matter of time before the collapse of this Fianna Fáil-Progressive Democrat government. Desmond O'Malley and Albert Reynolds had earlier given evidence to a tribunal of inquiry into the beef processing industry and its report highlighted critical conflicts between the politicians' contributions. Relationships between the two leaders quickly and publicly deteriorated, as accusations were traded at every opportunity.

The ensuing political storm saw the PDs leave government on 4 November 1992, ending what Albert

Reynolds had dismissed in an earlier speech as a 'temporary little arrangement'.

Lunching with my son Garrett in the Dáil restaurant that day, I was in rather a sombre mood, waiting to see Fine Gael party leader John Bruton to inform him that I would not be a candidate in the imminent election in the Dublin South constituency which I had represented since 1981. Having taken the decision to opt out of elected politics the previous summer, I had planned to inform the constituency organisation and John Bruton of my decision at the start of the new year, in anticipation of a 1993 general election.

It was a difficult decision to make. I was only fifty-seven, I was in a winnable seat and politics had been my career for over a decade, so why was I abandoning it now? My main reason was lack of challenge, also backbench isolation and a sense of a shift to the right both in the party and the Dáil. The fact that John Bruton was leader of Fine Gael also had a little to do with my decision.

I regretted that the snap general election brought all to a head as it did. I now had to break what I knew would be most unwelcome news to John. The meeting was tense. He was upset and, having failed to persuade me to reconsider my decision, he wished me well. I drafted the necessary press statement that I was standing down; the Fine Gael press office also issued a terse one. I returned to my seat in the Dáil chamber for the last time and listened to the final debate with its tributes to other retirees. Two of the towering figures of contemporary politics, Charles Haughey and Garret FitzGerald, were retiring after thirty-five and twenty-seven years respectively. Charles

Haughey had put his political epithet on the record on 11 February 1992 when he resigned as Taoiseach, claiming 'I have always sought to act solely and exclusively in the best interests of the Irish people. Let me quote *Othello*: "I have done the state some service: they know't, No more of that."'

I walked through the lobbies for the final time and colleagues offered good wishes and commiserations. Later that night, at a packed Fine Gael Constituency meeting in Mount Merrion, I explained my decision, thanked friends and colleagues for their friendship and support over the years and got a warm standing ovation.

There was some speculation at the time linking my opting out of politics with a much publicised late night protest by Youth Defence (a pro-life group) at my home in Dalkey the previous month. The young people, mainly third level students, were at the start of an anti-abortion political campaign and targeted me as the first victim. They came from the city in a van, all dressed in black. Their style was placards and a foot in the door and I found it extremely threatening as I was alone in our house, which is in a quiet complex. Shaken I may have been on the night but I recovered quickly and would never have yielded to such intimidation. My resignation was coincidence rather than a result of this protest.

I reflected that leaving politics voluntarily rather than losing a seat must be a little like leaving an enclosed religious order. One becomes bonded to the political family, which encompasses people from all parties. Time, energies and thinking were all about party politics, policies and strategies, with little time over for family or normal leisure pursuits. Walking away from Leinster House that day I felt some nostalgia and some relief but no regrets. I had lived in extraordinary political times since the exhilarating day in summer 1981 when I took my seat for the first time.

But as I left the precincts of Leinster House, I was not unaware of the implications of the coming election contest for my party colleagues and particularly for John Bruton. This was his first election as leader of Fine Gael. It was a personal challenge for him and a particularly difficult election for Fine Gael. That election cost the party ten seats, during which Fine Gael slumped to a national percentage of 24.5, the lowest since 1948.

On the other hand the 1992 election resulted in a historic breakthrough for the Labour Party under Dick Spring's leadership. Labour more than doubled their seats and for the first time, after long negotiations with other parties, went into government with Fianna Fáil. Members of Fine Gael, particularly John Bruton, took grave exception to this decision. The relationship between Dick Spring and John Bruton, which was never robust, was then at all-time low. There was a strange presumption among supporters of Fine Gael that their party was the only natural government partner for the Labour Party. Having shared government in 1973-7 and 1983-7, it seemed certain that the parties would team up again in the nineties. But it was not to be.

I was frankly amazed at the way in which Dick Spring bonded with Fianna Fáil in post-election negotiations, having listened so often in the Dáil chamber to his tongue-lashings of that party when he was in opposition just a few months previously. But politics is about nothing if not opportunity and timing and, having done his sums, Dick Spring reckoned a liaison with Fianna Fáil added up to stable government for four years at a time of promise in the economy.

2

Early Years

Not until I was five years old did I become aware of the serious job my father did. He arrested people, even locked them up, he stopped traffic by waving his hand, watched for enemy aircraft (it was 1941) and generally ensured that the people of the town of Portlaoise stayed safe and on the right side of the law. His job description, according to my mother, was 'sergeant-in-charge'. The charge involved twenty other Gardaí and a German shepherd dog, all housed in a rambling grey stone barracks on the Dublin Road. It was also home to the four of us Campbell children.

Previously it had been a British military barracks and little had been changed structurally in the forty years since Independence. Most impressive were the thirty-foot high stone perimeter walls and the gravel parade ground with its two black cannon. The girls' bedroom looked out on a small square, also overlooked by tiny barred cell windows. To us they were dungeons and when some unfortunate reveller spent the night there and roared or sang us to sleep, to us he was never less than a murderer or, better still, a kidnapper. It was here on the square that the Gardaí would line out for inspection and marching drill when the chief superintendent came to call, usually monthly.

Our home, the 'married quarters', was self-contained but on the dark side of the barracks. It owed nothing to comfort or modernity and our mother was never happy there. It had cold flagstone floors, no heating, high ceilings and big windows, all barred, whether to keep people in or out I am unsure. Out my mother always wanted and often, gazing through the bars at the light-blocking stone wall, would say to us, 'If I'd known this was where I'd end up, I'd have gone into a convent.' We were impervious to such fuss over a wall and loved our big, cosy kitchen. A solid black range dominated one side, which, fed on turf, had the water in the tank above the sink burping and gurgling by evening. A large painted dresser and big deal table and chairs left room for dolls, prams, bikes and train sets, even when the playpen came into occasional use.

But my mother, who was most undomesticated, was not won over by a warm kitchen. I imagine that the contrast with her single life of work, theatre and tennis while she was living with her family in Glasnevin, Dublin, must have been stark. Her only adult company was my father and when he talked about his work, it was with a caution not to gossip to other people. Cut off, without next-door neighbours like other wives, she was bored and restless and read numerous books from the local library. I imagine it was the only way she could escape the austerity of her life. Indeed she and all of us children must have been a little scarred by living in the barracks. I remember being sad for my mother: she did all the cooking, cleaning and shopping; she was weighed down. Young as I was, at around the age of ten, I questioned why she could not have changed her life, be a person as well as a mother. I resolved that motherhood alone would not be my destiny, a rather rebellious thought for the late 1940s!

Once every year we saw a different mum. Off she went to Dublin for a few days to see her father, with no children in tow. While there, with funds from her Dublin bank account, she hit the shops. Father met her off the Dublin train and this elegant figure, wafting perfume, with a new hairdo and make-up, scooped us up for hugs. One year she came home in a fur coat, with a black evening dress in the suitcase: it was for the Garda dinner dance, one of the black-tie social events held each year in the town.

Life for my mother did not get any easier. Two more brothers were born, in 1943 and 1945. Each birth was signalled for us children by the arrival of an elderly help, Mrs Martin from Dublin. She was no match for our energy and initiative and we loved the freedoms she enabled, even for a short time.

Wherever we lived, – and by 1941 he had been transferred six times – my father's passion was gardening. In the Portlaoise garden of lawn, roses and vegetables, he designed and made a swing and, rare indeed during the war years, we had our own strawberries which he cultivated. Although he left rural east Galway when he was twenty in 1922 to join An Garda Síochána, the values of country life like hospitality, conversation and a love of nature stayed with him forever.

He ran the barracks by the rule book and was tough on discipline and regulations. He seemed forever to be polishing his shoes, or putting polish on his jacket buttons, his hat badge and the brass stripes on his sleeve. I know he expected the same high standards from his colleagues and did not always get them, to hear him tell about 'that slovenly yoke from Roscommon'.

High standards were also set for us: we were told we were different from other children. We must always remember who our father was and never let him down. Even when I was very young I knew what that meant. When I was three I had let the whole family down. It was two years earlier when we lived in Kells and at three-and-a-half I was bundled off to school with my elder sister. On my second morning an argument developed between myself and the Sister of Mercy in charge of the infants' class. She had asked me to collect all the small writing boards in the class. But then she changed her mind. She would do it herself. But I held staunchly on to the boards. At three-and-a-half my vocabulary was poor, so to emphasise how I felt, I landed hefty (for a three-year-old) kicks on her shins. Word of my assault reached home before I did and I got a hiding and a lecture from my father. Next day was far worse. My dad brought me to school, he in full uniform, put me up on a table in class and made me apologise publicly for my attack. I so remember the humiliation I felt and during the rest of my schooldays never again felt comfortable with nuns.

At times, father decreed that there were certain children we should not associate with but he never said why. I often earwigged at night by the fire, as he told my mother about the awful people he dealt with in an area everyone called White City, a poor housing estate in Portlaoise. Its real name was O'Moore Place.

The inhabitants were portrayed as gangsters, criminals and drunks but in fact their lifestyle was related to the extreme deprivation of the day. It was an area of abject poverty. There were few jobs and even less social welfare for widows, children or the unemployed, such as we have today. There was endemic poverty, chronic lack of basics like food and heat, deprivation that robbed people of their self-esteem.

There was a general belief that poverty was self-induced. The poor were regarded as feckless and lazy and it was felt that poverty was unlikely to be eradicated. To help, people supported the St Vincent de Paul collections. Families like ours could feel secure because we had all the creature comforts. We never went barefoot or ill to school, we had warm clothes and good food and two parents, neither of whom ever came in 'footless drunk'. This was my father's normal depiction of drinkers whether after two pints or ten. A lifelong Pioneer, he would claim, 'Drink has never passed my lips.' He regarded alcohol as the root of all evil and the downfall of the young.

No other Garda carried out the 'bona fide' raids on public houses in the 1950s with the zeal of Paddy Campbell. According to after-hours or Sunday opening laws, publicans were legally allowed to serve alcohol only to 'travellers', people who had come a distance and could prove it. Local clients were barred. Most raids resulted in some arrests, visits to the district court, fines, names in the newspapers and other unwanted publicity.

We lived under a drink taboo in our house, constantly warned that it was something very bad indeed. I am not sure how attractive that made alcohol to my siblings, I was twenty-one before I drank wine but do remember being prudish around the subject.

On the one hand life in the barracks for us was confined and more than a little regimented but on the other hand the walls framed a safe imaginative playground. Outings were limited, to school at the local convent and home every day, or to the library and twice to church on Sundays. I recall only one trip to Dublin by train to visit an aunt. It was dangerous to complain of boredom to my mother, because there was always a pram for us girls to push. If our childhood was uneventful, happy and ordinary it was also desperately serious with little frivolity. Our home was an academy of duty, decency and self-sufficiency, of standards upheld and religion respected and well-practised.

We climbed, we skipped, we played hide and seek and we fought a good deal among ourselves. But the day of the year we lived for was St Patrick's Day. It was our Trooping Of the Colours with grandstand seats. The entire town paraded on 17 March. Pageants were scarce during the war and everyone from the smallest altar boy to the stoutest GAA official participated. With banners and uniforms came the Legion of Mary, the Children of Mary, the FCA, the GAA, boys' schools and girls' schools and every band for miles around. After two hours of raggle-taggle marching came the inspection and the salute was taken in the barrack yard – our barrack yard. Bigwigs and little wigs and the Campbell children passed unchallenged under the stone arch. Then the gates were shut and bolted.

Like the stormers of the Bastille the marchers outside

climbed walls and shoulders and squeezed heads and legs between bars. Meantime we sat in splendour on our garden fence, watching the military manoeuvres, not above sticking out a tongue at our erstwhile classmates.

While we had the freedom of the barrack square and environs, the day room and offices were strictly out of bounds to us children. But often a young Garda, a local boxing hero and owner of the German Shepherd dog, would come out and chase us or shadow box with us.

When, in April 1947, after seven years in Portlaoise, my father eventually got a transfer back to Dublin, Mother was blissfully happy. I imagine post-war Dublin was a pretty drab place but we were enthralled by our mother's idealised stories of it. To her it meant glamour and vitality: it was her London and New York all rolled into one. Although the official reason for the transfer from Portlaoise was 'congested married quarters', the small suburban semi-detached house we moved into in Dundrum was certainly not roomy. With only small front and back gardens, scope for any activity was very limited. My parents had bought the house when they were first married and now, with six children, intended it only as a short-stay home. We lived there for eight years.

But what compensations we discovered. A cinema across the road, shops, double-decker buses and joy of joy, other children to play with. Other changes for us were metered gas for cooking and ice cream shops. And our father no longer worked on the doorstep but went off like other fathers on his bicycle to the barracks every morning.

Once more we were enrolled in a new local school,

my third. The process of integration mid-term with other twelve year olds was daunting. It was more than the city/country divide or that I could just about understand the Dublin accents. It was about feeling an outsider and having to fight your corner to be heard. Having done so much barging in at new schools and girl guide patrols when young gave me a capacity to integrate and mix easily later on.

But it was soon back to convent life for me. In 1948 I followed my older sister into Dominican College, Eccles Street, as a day pupil. Though now gone from the streetscape, the college was then a splendid old building dedicated to the general education and spiritual needs of Irish girls. Like many women of my generation I was cocooned in an entirely female environment for my growing-up years.

To some extent I was starry-eyed because I liked belonging to and being identified with what was regarded as a good school. The identity involved a uniform, which was a black blazer with a pocket crest, a black-and-white scarf and a dark navy belted frock with a starched white collar. For our developing female shapes the box-pleated style was unfortunate. Big hips bulged disproportionately and pleats above the waist were never flattering for those girls unlucky (or lucky) enough to be first to develop big breasts.

I sorely wanted to be grown up and breasts meant you were on your way. But my hormones were either late or lazy and I remember thinking in my sixteenth year that I was destined for a flat-chested future. How I envied friends whose womanliness was poking through the navy box pleats. It is hard to understand now why we did not talk about any of this. And we didn't, not to parents, teachers, who were mainly nuns, nor one another, and there was no reading material, not even magazines for reference. Ironically such books would not have been allowed under our censorship laws.

Everything related to sex was taboo. Despite the hormonal earthquakes we were all experiencing and despite the numerous questions for which we had no answers, we had to cope alone. Did the curriculum involve information or discussion about menstruation, pregnancy, relations with boys? Not at all, not in any shape, because in those different times there was a belief that ignorance of the facts of life kept girls out of trouble. 'Getting into trouble' was the shorthand for unmarried pregnancy. Blame when it happened never attached to the male involved; the unfortunate girl and her family had to live with hostility and shame. Many girls were spirited away to the UK for an anonymous confinement and in most cases had their babies adopted in England. The Irish value system of the time certainly robbed women not only of basic choices but of fundamental rights.

Choices in education scarcely existed. By this I mean that we were not encouraged to be career-minded. For us girls, life would not involve serious work like that of an airline pilot, a politician or a surgeon. In general the teaching of mathematics and science in girls' schools was totally inadequate. Indeed there was a tradition and a belief that women were not 'naturally' good at mathematics and science. I am not sure how much this educational policy had to do with job scarcity and a bias towards the employment of men, as was the case in later years. The natural order was that women married and had several children and required only interim employment after school. Jobs could be found in the traditional women's sector, whether as a secretary, a nurse or a teacher – or if you were pretty and lucky as an air hostess. A university qualification was simply not an objective and no one inspired us with ideas of academic success or achievement.

Girls' schools were therefore in harmony with Irish society. All across the spectrum of home, school and church, the perception of the role of women was crystal-clear and unchallenged. Women were caring, domestic creatures, needing protection, guidance and understanding for their nervous and emotional personalities. Back then, opportunity and equality mattered not at all. Unlike other European countries, most Irish married women were not in gainful employment. We had no industrial revolution, no post-war recovery to spur change.

The worse aspect was that most girls and women passively accepted this image. All the way through convent school we were drip-fed the story of the Virgin Mary. We heard about the virgin birth before we knew what either word meant. If this did not fix our social expectations, the early indoctrination of Adam and Eve in the Garden of Eden did. Eve was formed from Adam's rib and she then made Adam eat the forbidden apple, thereby condemning mankind to sin for ever more. It was a heavy burden of guilt and responsibility to bear, when all we wanted was to be beautiful, to grow up quickly and fall in love.

At a particular stage in fourth year certain girls were selected for the Children of Mary sodality. I am not sure what criterion was applied except that, unlike my sister, I did not qualify. As a Child of Mary, exemplary and virtuous behaviour was expected but you also got to wear a medal on a blue ribbon with a pale blue satin cloak on special occasions and you had the right to be buried in it when you died.

Before leaving Eccles Street I took a one-year secretarial course which included English, Shorthand and Typing, and graduated with some incredible speed like 100 words per minute in Pitman shorthand. I recall my English teacher – a nun – although not her name, who encouraged me greatly in writing. I got to read out my essays in her class, which was a nice boost.

Career counselling was non-existent: after all you were destined to become a typist and what more was there to be said. As expected my father helped to sort us out, sending me into a tea-importing firm on Bachelor's Walk and my older sister Bernie into Power's Distillery. My offices would not have been out of place in the era of Dickens: glass-panel doors, scrubbed wooden and tiled floors and counters with opening shutters. You would call it a respectable place to work but it was dull and boring and I never got beyond typing forms and stock recording.

Then one weekend, things changed. I met Brian Fennell at Templeogue Tennis Club. He worked nearby, across the Liffey, in his father's office and he owned a motorbike. My future lit up. Even then I felt that our lives would run in tandem. How right I was.

It was clear that economically Ireland was not going anywhere fast and the push and pull effect of emigration was influencing many young people. The pull effect was that countries like Canada and Australia began canvassing for workers and offered them travel subsidies, while the push included the chronic unemployment, low wages and poor prospects in Ireland at that time. So Brian and I opted to go to Canada.

3

A 1950s Emigrant

Newly engaged in the summer of 1957, Brian and I left Ireland for a new life in Montreal, Canada. Behind us we left a country of sepia tones, dark and grainy, of uncertain futures and real frugality.

When we decided to emigrate it was no surprise to relatives and friends because young people were on the move as never before. For my father, though, it was a shock. He was desolate and regarded our emigration as his failure. Late one night when everyone else was in bed, I discovered him crying by the fireside. After all, he reasoned, Brian and I both had jobs as clerks, he in his father's insurance brokerage, myself in a tea and wine merchants. In the thinking of parents of the time, if you got on the job ladder, worked hard and kept out of trouble, you could be made for life. Father's idea of achievement was a permanent job and acceptance into the company pension scheme (I was twenty-one at this time). But it was not mine, I had goals and visions I could not share with him.

I knew that his expectations were moulded by his life's experience. Growing up on a smallholding in east Galway, he knew first-hand about emigrants who left and never came back. While he danced and sang at the American wakes around the townland of Lisheenavarnogue, he also witnessed the void left afterwards for parents and siblings. Bitter tears were shed for many weeks and months. His generation dealt stoically with emigration. It was almost inevitable in every rural family. It was painful and it was permanent. Not so with us, I assured him: we'd return in two or three years and would certainly come back to get married. Though this was poor consolation it improved his outlook.

My spirits soared as we filled in the many forms necessary to meet the emigrant requirements of the Canadian government. These included chest x-rays, full medicals and applications for work visas. Being the first to leave our large family, saying good-bye to family and relatives was tough but it was overlaid by feelings of escape at last. Somehow it didn't seem proper to anticipate new horizons so strongly but I knew I wanted away from a stifled, narrow-minded Ireland. I would take my chances and bring my youthful optimism and energy to a place of opportunity and tolerance.

And to a country with none of the high moral guardianship of public behaviour which was a fixation of Irish governments then. Not long before we left home *The Irish Times* had reported Labour Party Leader and Minister for Social Welfare Brendan Corish at a meeting in Wexford saying: 'We ought to pay tribute to the type of censorship we have and jealously guard it.' (2 June 1956) Three months previously a ban had been imposed on the circulation of the UK newspaper *The Observer* because it contained an article on family planning. Where we were headed these tentacles of repression would not reach.

We landed in Montreal fourteen hours after leaving Ireland. There were tears and farewells from extended family, first at Dublin and then at Shannon airports, where we boarded a KLM propeller aircraft. It stopped for lengthy periods at both Gander and Idlewild airports.

All exhaustion disappeared at my first glimpse of the city of Montreal. It was love at first sight. We were confronted by a vision of glittering lights, noise and people everywhere. Wafting at us was the balmy warmth of a North-American June night. The summer of 1957 unfolded for Brian and me as an adventure of discovery, all of it fascinating. We were experiencing another way of life, a vastly different culture, more liberal than Ireland. Most of it we liked. We were hedged against homesickness, having each other to share new experiences with. Our first weeks were spent with my cousin, Sligo-born Tom Campbell and his wife. As relatives abroad do, he created space in his small apartment to accommodate us, despite having two very young children. He lived in an upmarket Jewish neighbourhood called Mount Royal, only minutes from downtown Montreal by streetcar. Under Tom's guidance we came to grips with the food, the currency and the transport system. Also new for us was the bilingualism, although French was not as widely spoken then in Quebec province as it is now.

We both got jobs almost immediately, working in different departments of the massive Sun Life Insurance building in central, leafy Dominion Square. I had status beyond my expectations, as private secretary to a finance director and a bright twentieth-floor office all to myself. Somehow, having a secretary from the 'old world' gave my boss status. Clients and other contacts would phone long distance 'just to hear your accent'. In truth I recall little shamrockery and my Sun Life boss was a genial, grey-haired sixty-year-old. That is not to say we were not referred to as DPs (displaced persons) now and again. Being perceived as homeless or displaced (with regard to our country) hit a raw nerve and brought out a fierce national pride in me. In Canada's potpourri population of Ukrainians, Poles, Chinese, Icelanders, Swedes, Italians, English and Dutch, being Irish was nothing special. In fact the immigration situation in Canada in the mid-1950s was the same as in the United States a hundred years before. Canada needed people to fill jobs in their booming economy. One Montreal daily paper carried twelve columns of jobs, from advertising executives and secretaries to cooks and drivers.

For the many Hungarians who in 1957 really were displaced persons, being called DPs was a sad reminder of their tragic homeland. After the revolution of 1956, Canada took in thousands of Hungarian refugees, many escaping by the skin of their teeth. Being unable to speak either English or French and coping with life in a capitalist society, where the state did not take care of them, was isolating indeed. The Hungarians were mostly young men who were deeply traumatised by the invasion of their country, the violence in their streets and their worry about family left behind.

After I moved jobs from Sun Life to Canadian Railway for better pay if less status, I rented a room in the Mount

Royal area in an old house run by a delightful Hungarian couple called Lillica and Lotzi Simonzy. Lotzi, who was in his late sixties, left the house daily with a fat briefcase and wearing a tie, to work in a warehouse, while Lillica, Lotzi's second wife, who could only speak a little English, ran the guesthouse and was a wonderful cook.

We did a deal with her: a tiny room and breakfast for me and an evening meal for both Brian and me. No, we did not live together, which was a major puzzle to all our Canadian friends. I suppose we were imbued with the mores of Ireland fifty years ago and we never even discussed it! Brian rented a dark little room nearer the city. Other guests in my house were Jack, a wheezy elderly chain-smoking Canadian, who had served a lengthy jail term, and an African-American draft dodger called Jeff.

But the ones we got to know best were Norbert and Erno, refugees from Budapest. At table they pored over the most lurid tabloids – 'Bishop impregnates choir girl' type of headline – ruefully explaining that this was part of their English language class! As their English improved we had numerous animated discussions and found strong similarities between Ireland and Hungary, both historical and cultural. The Simonzys created a home from home for all of us. Lillica was both beautiful and kind, and inspired affection and support amongst us. As well as that it was a safe haven for dissecting and analysing life in this new and amazing country which had adopted us.

So fast was I absorbing new experiences, different customs and practices in the first months in Montreal, that I wanted to slow it all down. Not possible: you either kept pace or were left behind. Emerging from an unsophisticated 1950s Ireland where televisions and telephones were still luxuries and our tallest building was Imco Cleaners on Dublin's Merrion Road, we were awe-struck on a daily basis.

Canadian homes were a revelation: bright and warm, a TV in every room, gleaming modern kitchens and bathrooms and the inevitable enormous cars in every drive. Petrol then cost mere cents a gallon.

Shopping was a pure delight: the diversity of consumer goods was unimaginable and Steinbergs supermarkets were everything the Irish corner grocery shop had never been. And from my first trip to downtown stores like Morgans, Etons and Oglyvies I became a serial browser. I spent many after-work hours in these enormous consumer cathedrals, which were cool in summer and warm in winter and right away decided I needed some spending money. Not that I could imagine shopping like many of the Canadian women I knew at work who bought dresses by twos, sweaters by fours. It was the same in their homes, where nothing lasted long enough to wear out. On a whim out went the curtains, the floor covering, the lights, the chairs, the dishes even, in favour of a completely new decor. Surprisingly it was not a cash society: there were store cards, credit cards, instalment payments and bank loans and most people were very candid about their borrowings. Strange for someone coming from a country where buying items on the never-never (hire purchase) was a closely-guarded secret, even a bit shady.

One of the joys of Montreal was that bits of it seemed just like a French town, while other aspects were pure American. We took all in our stride: the sixteen inches of snow in winter, the obsession with ice hockey, the contrast between five degrees below and central heating temperatures of seventy-five degrees or more. At the beginning I wanted everyone I knew and loved to come to Canada. They just did not know what they were missing!

We made great friends. The home of the Irish family of Martin Beausang was a hub for many newly arrived emigrants. Both the children and parents were very hospitable and we had party evenings but also nights of arguments and music. The Beausangs' door was always open and a beer on offer.

An office colleague, Dora Rusicia, became a lifelong friend. Her parents had come from Sicily as newlyweds and prospered in Montreal. Because her mother never learned English we could not talk, but her kindness knew no bounds. With Dora and her friends we developed a wonderful Canadian outdoor life, winter and summer. My first ski lessons were on wooden skis with leather boots in the Laurentian mountains.

We set our wedding date for 29 October 1958. We married in Dublin and were sad to leave Montreal and our friends. We were unsure if we would return to Canada or stay and try and make a go of working in Dublin. Rumours said the Irish economy was promising and things were looking up. Or maybe we just wanted to believe this, because, back with family and friends we realised how much we had missed them. We both got jobs fairly easily: Brian in a Dublin life insurance company with a salary of £500 per year, myself in a legal firm, which was strictly a stop-gap position.

My in-laws were rather unhappy that I was working: married women just did not work in the 1950s. Deciding to remain in Dublin, we bought a three-bedroom house with mountain views and a car. Then we had our first daughter. Her birth was the most fulfilling and wonderful experience of my life. Even winning a Dáil seat does not come near it.

But politics were a long way off. My life was now totally domesticated: cooking, cleaning, polishing, shopping. Was this the process of 'settling down'? Would I now be content and normal like other mothers? Two more babies, a son and a daughter, arrived, to keep me busy. Of course I had to feel I was a perfect mother. But memories of my mother in her barrack kitchen and her ill-concealed frustrations were very strong during those years. I was like a gasket ready to blow when Brian came in from work. All I wanted was to talk to a grown-up and discuss current affairs. I even told Brian how I felt, which was more than I could do to other adults. Firstly no other mother I knew felt like I did and secondly the older generation would have seen it as unlucky to be talking like that with such a wonderful husband and three lovely children. Therein lay the trap.

4

A Feminist Awakening

It was 1970. I had been married twelve years. It seemed a lifetime, although I was only thirty-five. Like other husbands on our road, Brian disappeared every day into early-morning traffic and returned home at teatime. Only one woman on our road joined this exodus. Some mornings I watched her. A married woman who worked! Lighting a cigarette, she would walk to the bus stop at the same time every morning, perfectly made-up, earrings, high heels and bright with expectation. What liberation and joy that seemed, except that I felt sorry for her too. I knew she had no children. According to the convention of the day women could not have both a job and a family. So mothers like me stayed home, to live the 'happy ever after' promise of novels and women's magazines. We tried to inject excitement and fulfilment into the days of housework and shopping. But diversions like coffee mornings and trips to the supermarket only reinforced my sense of worthless non-personhood.

As did RTÉ morning radio, where commentators, all men, Gay Byrne, Liam Nolan, Rodney Rice and Mike Murphy talked at us. Women wrote confessional letters to them – and after hearing some poignant letter from a lonely abused mother of ten, you felt your life was not too bad after all. That feeling did not last long.

Formal childcare as we know it today in shopping centres, work places and local communities did not exist. So with three nearby mothers, friends with toddlers of the same age as mine, I improvised a rota of play mornings.

As one of the foot soldiers in the vast army of suburban housewives in the 1960s and 1970s, I felt invisible, irrelevant and in a role from which I wanted escape. Not escape from Brian and the children whom I loved dearly, but from the domestic cell of tedious repetition and the sense of being brain-dead. For me it was stop the world: I want to get on.

Seriously questioning the Irish norm for wives as against the norm for husbands and looking at how this could be changed was a tall order in 1970. It meant questioning our education, our labour laws and our lack of childcare facilities but even more than this, it meant challenging long-held public perceptions about women as wives and mothers. I began by buying a second-hand portable typewriter and started writing articles about marriage, careers and women's education for the women's pages of the newspapers, such as the *Irish Press* and *Evening Press,* and for RTÉ feature programmes. Once I began to be published regularly I got a significant amount of feedback. I discovered a large audience of women equally frustrated and impatient with their lives. Their only nugget of hope was that they would find a voice.

It was through this journalistic work that I became acquainted with the women who made up the Irish

Women's Liberation Movement. It was to be the seedbed of many new organisations in the 1970s and 1980s, from which legislative reforms and social change for women would eventually flow.

As organisations go, the Irish Women's Liberation Movement was a strange animal, more a flash of feminist defiance than a conventional movement. It burst on an unsuspecting Ireland in 1970, only to peter out the following year. During that short time it delivered a fierce wallop to the conventions of the time around the role of women in Irish life. It challenged, as no other group had done before, the expectations that society had of women. It shocked and outraged religious and political opinion and it gave women a voice and a visibility for the first time.

Irish Women's Liberation started with a small number of women – Margaret Gaj, Mary Maher, Máirín Johnston, Doctor Máire Woods and Máirín de Búrca – who met in Bewleys Café in Westmoreland Street in Dublin. Most of these women had already been involved in left-wing activities during the 1960s and, motivated by reports from the US of a new, radical women's movement, they discussed how such a movement might be introduced into Ireland.

Early meetings of the original group were held in an upstairs room in Margaret Gaj's restaurant in Baggot Street. Then as numbers grew the venue moved to Mary Maher's house and, later, when I became involved, meetings were in Mary Kenny's apartment in Ballsbridge.

Mary Kenny, who was women's editor of the *Irish*

Press in 1971, was my conduit to feminist politics. As a freelance journalist I wrote regularly for her newspaper and for the *Evening Press,* whose features editor Sean McCann published my first articles. Mary Kenny was very keen for me to come to Women's Liberation meetings but in those days I was not a joiner. I was a busy thirty-five-year-old mother of three small children, working as a freelance writer, and from what I knew of it Women's Liberation seemed little more than a fad. Because I spent my evenings writing, they were too precious to me to spend at meetings. But Mary's power of persuasion was such that I relented and went to my first meeting, thereby changing the course of my whole life.

Mary Kenny and I went on an assignment together at the new ESB works at Turlough Hill in Wicklow. During the drive home we talked shop, discussing future features for the paper and how the women's page could best reflect the life of women at the time. We talked about the tragic letters we both got from women, and our sense of helplessness in the face of the institutional injustice many suffered: cases like the young mother of three children in County Roscommon who had a heart complaint and who had been told by the doctor not to get pregnant again under any circumstances. She knew she needed reliable contraception but neither doctor nor chemist could help her and her husband wanted to leave things in the hands of God.

It happened that there was a Women's Liberation meeting due the following night, at which a detailed report on discrimination was being drafted, and Mary pleaded with me to come and help. So I went – but timidly. When I arrived, Mary's apartment was dark and very smoky. It was full of strange women, who were not over-friendly. Everyone spoke at once and argued aggressively. Some faces I recognised from television or from columns in *The Irish Times* or the *Irish Independent*. I felt a fundamental gap between the group and myself. Most were single women with professional careers, at the other end of the spectrum from this suburban housewife, mother and freelance hack. I listened to all the voices at once but the housewife in me wondered if I would be better occupied in the kitchen washing Mary's sink of dirty dishes.

But as the night went on I got hooked – intrigued and fascinated by the views and opinions of the women. This truly was where I wanted to be. I stayed until well after midnight, totally absorbed. It was my introduction to the Irish Women's Liberation Movement.

Brian remembers that night clearly. I came home very late reeking of cigarette smoke. I woke him and talked about the meeting and about the women I had met. We talked into the early hours. I told him that these women were a revelation to me, serious women talking a language I had not heard before, sharing their journeys to personal liberation. It was my first consciousness-raising experience. Not once were children or cleaning the oven mentioned. It was all vastly different from the conventional women's world that I occupied. None of these women lived in my designated women's zone of daily caring and cleaning and what was more they did not even seem to know about it.

I went back the next week and began to contribute

to the debate. Many of the women delved into their personal experiences and quite openly spoke about their lives. I heard a catalogue of misery, of violent and drunken fathers, ruthless bosses, unmarried motherhood, unfaithful husbands and abortions – until I began to wonder if I was some sort of freak, having so far had what I regarded as a contented and conventional life.

In the group, discussion could be passionate and angry. Often it was open season on men and if anyone (me) objected to the anti-man rhetoric, some women present questioned one's credentials and disputed one's commitment to feminism. It was even suggested to me that I join the Irish Countrywomen's Association, where I would have no problem with radical thinking.

At first I found this collective scape-goating of men very difficult. I was uncomfortable with the anti-man thrust of many in the group, although I empathised with the grievances. I pointed out that it was inaccurate and unfair to lob grenades at all men and if we were to pursue the social and legal changes so urgently needed, men's cooperation and support would be necessary. Why adopt such an alienating approach? But I was in a minority on this. I realised I sounded preachy, decided this kind of criticism was par for any women's lib course and quit defending men.

Despite the arguments, the differences between us and the lack of organisation, we made progress. For instance there were neither agendas nor minutes of meetings, for which the chairperson rotated weekly. But in early 1970 we produced a concise report called *Irish Women, Chains or Change*. In thirty–one pages it documented the reality of life for Irish women at home and at work and drew up five demands for action:

- equal pay
- equality before the law
- equal education opportunities
- contraception
- justice for deserted wives, widows and unmarried mothers

The report spelled out in some detail the widespread discrimination suffered by women under the Irish Constitution and under our legal system. It was launched amidst extensive media coverage and it galvanised many women into action. Thousands contacted us, wanting to identify and be involved with the group and urging on the campaign. We felt we had hit the right note.

Many women began to question their roles both in the home and at work. The message went right to the core of most women's lives. Not by a long shot did all women approve of this message: there was bitter and vocal opposition from some. At the same time many Irish men regarded the Women's Liberation Movement as a joke, many even making ribald comments about the women involved. It was the last thing on their minds that the 1970 campaign was the bell tolling on their traditional positions in Irish society.

During 1970 the bestselling feminist book, Betty Friedan's *The Feminine Mystique*, first published in the US in 1963, became available in Ireland, and thousands of women read it. For many housewives it struck a chord.

On page 331, Friedan unravelled the concept of the 'happy housewife':

> Who knows what women can be when they are
> finally free to become themselves? Who knows
> what women's intelligence will contribute when
> it can be nourished without denying love?
> Who knows of the possibilities of love when
> men and women share not only children, home
> and garden, not only the fulfilment of their
> biological roles but the responsibilities and
> passions of the work that creates the human
> future. It has barely begun, the search of women
> for themselves.

This was heady stuff and my well-thumbed copy of *The Feminine Mystique* was read, reread and then loaned to another woman.

Friedan was writing about the US experience but her book applied to wives and mothers throughout the western world. Other women gurus appeared: in the UK Australian-born Germaine Greer published *The Female Eunuch* in 1970 and Simone de Beauvoir's classic *The Second Sex*, which had been banned in Ireland until 1970, became available in English. Many women read all the feminist literature they could get their hands on. They discussed and debated it among themselves and began to reject the theory that biology dictated the destiny of women. The women's revolution had arrived!

I continued to attend Women's Liberation meetings. One night someone defined the 'new woman'. She would be financially and emotionally independent of men. She would not be cooking for them, ironing their shirts or cleaning their homes: there would be an end to the slavery of contemporary marriage. Furthermore, new woman could be her natural self, no longer needing make-up, hairdos, sexy underwear and all the other embellishments women used to please men. Help! I thought – what about wearing them to please *us*? But no, all would go; new woman would present her natural unadorned self to the world. Oh dear, was I to be out of step with the group on this one too? I could not be enthusiastic about any of this and thought what a drab unexciting colourless vision it created. But I was still more than a little intimidated by it all and didn't want to appear too much of the traditional woman. I definitely dressed down going to meetings and rubbed off the lipstick and eye shadow before going in.

That is until I saw June Levine arriving in purple suede knee-high laced-up boots and a tight-fitting black dress. Divorced and recently returned from Canada with three small children, June seemed older, wiser and certainly more sophisticated than most of us. Her book *Sisters*, published in 1982, covers in a moving and very personal way her life and marriage and deals with the Irish Women's Liberation Movement from her perspective.

As time went on, I immersed myself in the group's feminist vision of the future and week-by-week began finding answers to the dilemmas of my Irish Catholic girlhood. It was both exciting and frightening. As girls we had been socialised to feel we had little value: education was not regarded as an imperative for us as it was for boys. After all, *they* would be the breadwinners. This second-class socialisation was to follow us through life, in the family, in school, at work, in marriage, always in the long shadow of the Catholic hierarchy, which asserted its right to influence the government policies that shaped our world.

No one, not politicians, not social planners, not even women themselves, questioned why the Church should have such an influence on important and intimate aspects of women's lives. I knew many women who lived lives of quiet desperation, emotionally deprived in their marriages or having far too many pregnancies, but they were powerless to influence anything.

Women were compelled to leave public-sector employment on marriage and thereafter were financially dependent on their husbands. Irish women, particularly married women, were, according to state laws and regulations, unworthy of responsibility. Even to borrow a library book one needed a husband's signature, as one did to get a bank loan, or to claim the children's allowance which was paid by the state.

There were no female judges, pilots, bus drivers or jurors. Women's principal occupations were as factory workers, clerks, shop assistants, domestics, nurses, laundry workers and waitresses, all low-paid and low-status work. Women earned approximately 45 per cent of men's wages for the same work. This was just the way life was ordered in the Ireland of the 1970s. Some of these inequalities were due to deliberate and active legal discrimination tolerated over time: others reflected custom and tradition.

The net result was the same: Irish women were segregated into very specific roles, which appeared irredeemably fixed. I began to understand the stress and frustration I so often felt, as a result of being classified a housewife. I now understood the strains I had noticed in my mother's life as we were growing up.

Her single life in Dublin as a well-paid secretary, enjoying tennis, theatre and travel, was transformed after her marriage at the age of twenty-nine to a life of financial dependence, of having six children in ten years and living in the suffocating narrowness of a country town. But for the fact that my parents' marriage was a loving one and my father a kind and patient man, my mother's life (and ours) would certainly have been much worse.

Nonetheless the desperation I observed – her sense of entrapment and her lack of control over her life, seeped into my very being. As a small child I wanted no part of it and told whoever would listen that I was going to be a man when I grew up. I knew this type of lifestyle was not for me but at that time there were no choices: girls just became wives, then mothers, then grannies – and that was it. You took on the chores appropriate to each stage. Your aim was to be the best: wife, mother and granny. The sequence of events for women was preordained and involved a lifetime of repetitious chores inside the house.

As the meetings in Mary Kenny's apartment I was more of an observer than a contributor. I found the women exhilarating and energising, although at first people like Nell McCafferty and Máirín de Búrca seemed quite intimidating. Máirín was then a Sinn Féin party activist, who regularly featured in newspaper reports of street demonstrations on issues related to the Northern

Ireland Troubles. I felt that I had little in common with her: she was very serious, single-minded and angry and appeared to disapprove of the rest of us and regard us as frivolous. Máirín was committed to the global revolution for which, she intimated, we should all fight and as part of which women would get their liberation. I never bought into that, I'm afraid, but Máirín de Búrca, more than most members of the Women's Liberation group, won a historic victory for women. In 1974 Máirín along with Mary Anderson, challenged the constitutionality of the 1927 Juries Act and won the right for women to serve on juries. Subsequently the law on jury selection was amended, from a choice from among twelve male property owners to one among all men and women on the register of electors.

The Irish Times journalist Nell McCafferty was another high-profile woman whom I found challenging. When Nell came to meetings, she could dominate an entire evening. She was dogmatic and loud but very funny. When she became animated, which was often the case, her rich Derry accent would become so emphasised that no one knew what she was saying. Her column in *The Irish Times*, 'In the Eyes of the Law', was a daily chronicle of how the poor and marginalised fared in our courts. It was some time before I realised she was a lesbian, which was not easy in Ireland in 1970.

For me and for other women, the Irish Women's Liberation Movement *was* Mary Kenny. The media regarded her as the organisation's spokesperson and this drove other members into a fury at meetings. Mary's reputation was legendary. She smoked, she drank, she wore hot pants and large hats with feathers and flowers on them, often all at the same time and while riding a bike and smoking a long-stemmed pipe. For me, Mary, who drew so many women into the Women's Liberation web, was an icon. She was never boring; she was warm and generous and great fun. Not for her an apology or an excuse for her behaviour. Mary told everyone how to live and how to rear their children. She had a devastating honesty, which the media loved, and a probing curiosity.

At my first meeting with Mary in the lounge of the Shelbourne Hotel, Dublin, she looked me in the eye and asked when I had last had sex and with whom. A bit off-putting really for a respectable married Catholic woman with three children. But that was Mary! She set out to shock and mostly she succeeded.

Her women's page in the *Irish Press* was the most readable on the scene at the time. She cultivated and published women writers like myself, Mavis Arnold, Ginny Kennerley, Rosita Sweetman, Terry Prone and Linda Kavanagh, and gave us freedom to cover controversial, even unpopular issues.

After two years with the *Irish Press*, writing about and espousing the cause of women's rights, Mary left Dublin rather suddenly. She went back to London, having accepted the position of features editor of the *Evening Standard*. The *Irish Press* was none too happy with her decision. Having hit the conservative *Press* group like a tornado and dealt with the angst she created in the conventional readership, she was beginning to be regarded as an asset to circulation. The dilemma was: who could follow Mary Kenny? She had brought the women's page to dizzy new heights and the question was: who could keep it there? The *Irish Press* chose to go to the other extreme. Mary's successor as women's editor was a conservative journalist and broadcaster called Liam Nolan. A skilled and experienced writer, Liam was regarded as a safe pair of hands and very unlikely to upset the Catholic Church.

Many of Mary's feminist colleagues felt let down at her departure, at a point when the women's movement was beginning to take off. I was glad for her; the new job was considerable promotion. I felt she owed nothing to us and was in fact practising what we had all been preaching. What subsequently did cause anger and upset to a great number of Irish women was Mary's apparent revisionism. After she went to live in London, she appeared to rediscover Catholicism and domesticity and began writing critically about Women's Liberation. She was also very critical of her own behaviour when she was in her twenties. That she announced these changes of opinion very publicly, on radio and television, in magazines and in religious journals was regrettable and for me very difficult to understand. Mary was now married with two sons. In the space of ten years she had performed a full about-turn.

In the *AIM Group Magazine* of June 1980 Mary Kenny wrote:

> The problem itself for women lies in this double-edged gift of expanded opportunities.
>
> Sure it is marvellous to read about women cabinet ministers, women lawyers, women bankers, women engineers and to realise,

thereby, that any woman can nowadays get to the top of any profession that she chooses. At the same time, every time you praise the achievement of the women lawyer or the woman airline pilot, you are in a subtle way, putting down the less dazzling achievements of the woman who is spending her time at home with her family.

In the following issue of the magazine of September-December 1980 a reader, Margaret Dolan, responded to the article:

Well, I'm not going back to my little box with its little woman label. I am older now and wiser and, dare I say, liberated, insofar as I have the choice to stay or not to stay at home with my children. I choose to stay and choice breeds contentment. Anyway, Mary, it must be nice to have seen it all, done it all, written it all and when the well dries up, change sides. I know I'm being harsh but I'm just trying to figure out whether Mary is a renegade or a convert. Or is it just a matter of timing?

Although I have known Mary Kenny very well over all the years from 1970 and never once doubted her sincerity during the era of the Irish Women's Liberation Movement, I have ever fathomed what changed her so dramatically and so dogmatically. This created confusion and disappointment for many women still in transition to change. For me it mattered not at all. My life and my focus had changed and I had no doubt that the feminist principles of equal treatment and equal participation which had been valid ten years before were still valid. I did not agree with Mary Kenny on many important issues and still don't, but we don't let it affect our friendship

Women's liberation was about women other than Mary Kenny and myself. Eimear Philbin Bowman was one of the quiet, reasonable voices at the meetings and someone I felt I could work with; I remember she was pregnant at the time. Rosita Sweetman, author of *On Our Knees,* and a contributor to the *Irish Press* Women's Page was terribly impatient and seemed to argue all the time about everything. Fionnuala O'Connor was a schoolteacher from Northern Ireland and always came with her close friend, printer Marie McMahon. *The Irish Times* journalist, American-born Mary Maher, who was involved right from the beginning, had a deep and constant commitment to the movement and wrote challengingly on women's issues. Bernadette Quinn, a pharmacist and writer, and her sister Máire Humphreys were already part of the group when I joined. Dubliner Máirín Johnston, who was a Labour Party activist and trade unionist, was also one of the founding group. Máirín was warm and good-humoured and brought a practical dimension to discussions, which I think had to do with the fact that she was married with children.

Early on the founding group took a decision that there would be no hierarchical structure in Women's Liberation: no leaders, just a rotating chair for meetings and no agendas. It was all to be hassle-free with no grasping for power and all would have equal status in the group. A beautiful concept, which reputedly worked in the US, but in my view a concept for disaster, if longevity was the aim.

While structure and order may have been missing at our meetings, and discussions often went off in diverse directions, we talked freely, we argued and we shared experiences and in the process released energy and suppressed emotion. Meetings were an oasis of trust and mutual support. They released considerable frustration, anger and pain about the condition of Irish women, in many cases pain of a very personal nature.

We speculated about how much change we wanted. Should we or could we radically alter society, even seek alternatives to the nuclear family? What about the fashion and cosmetic industries that so manipulated women? What to do about the Catholic Church that oppressed women? The list was long but our first focus was the fundamentals, changes that would actually improve life for ordinary women. We should have a choice of contraception, be able to get divorced when marriages broke down, have equal pay and equal job opportunity. Our discussion on social engineering even included artificial insemination. Male domination in all its manifestations had to be challenged and power shared equally.

But nothing was going to be that easy. For a start we could not agree among ourselves on a common approach. This was really not too surprising, given the rainbow nature of the group politically. The socialists and Marxists amongst us inevitably wanted to go for bottom-up revolution, joining with other mainstream left-wing organisations, while the middle-class reformers like myself vehemently opposed this, arguing for systemic change.

While the majority of women in the group were serious radicals and activists, others were prepared to go along for the ride and excitement. Those of us who were social reformers were in the minority and became isolated. We began to be regarded as a bit of a pain. I earnestly believed that we needed to keep the women's campaign very clear and specific, separate and focused, with realistic aims. We should not, I was convinced, subsume our efforts and objectives under the broader revolutionary banner, which at that time included Northern Ireland, housing, unemployment and health. For me it was very much: 'Roll your sleeves up time, clarify the objectives and target the political institutions.'

After the publication of our charter of rights, *Irish women – Chains or Change* and the resulting publicity, we had to take serious stock of what we stood for. Letters came pouring in to our post office box, awful disclosures from unhappy women all over the country. Some women sent us money, many told us they supported what we were doing and encouraged us to keep it up. Amidst this positive response, I began to wonder at our ability to deliver. I asked: did we not need to give some lead and develop a strategy to bring the campaign to another stage?

A few of the women, especially June Levine and Mary Kenny, were impatient to go public and hoped to make Women's Liberation a popular national organisation.

Most of the founder group argued against this. Mary Kenny, an ardent newspaper woman, just wanted to publicise the movement, and for her the bigger the headlines the better. For Mary, nothing existed until it was written and talked about.

Much to the fury of most of the others, Mary talked to Pan Collins, a researcher for RTÉ's highly rated *Late Late Show*. According to Mary Kenny it was a chance encounter with Pan but some doubted this. I felt it made sense, if we hoped to move to a national platform, to appear on the television programme with the biggest audience.

The outcome was that compère Gay Byrne promised an entire programme on Women's Liberation, which could be our showcase to the country. Our organisation had a firm hand in structuring the programme. For the first time ever on television there was to be an all-woman panel: Senator Mary Robinson, Maynooth lecturer Mary Cullen, television producer Lelia Doolan, trade unionist Máirín Johnson and journalist Nell McCafferty, while the audience would be sprinkled with feminists and representatives of women's organisations.

On 6 March 1971 most of the group arrived at RTÉ's television studio in a definite climate of history in the making. A moderate tone was maintained during the panel discussion. However, Gay Byrne then invited the studio audience to participate and the temperature rose. In the heat of the discussion Mary Kenny, sitting in the front row of the audience, proclaimed that Irish legislators would resist change for women, because they frankly did not give a damn about women's rights. The temperature rose further and programme planning and structure went out the studio window.

A prominent politician was sitting at home by his fireside and heard Mary Kenny's accusation. Being who he was, he decided he had to challenge her. Opposition front-bench TD Garret FitzGerald was so stung by Mary's remarks that he got into his car and came straight over to the RTÉ studio. During a commercial break, in an unprecedented move, he was ushered straight to studio and on to the all-woman panel. There was no consultation or discussion with us women about the change, and the programme took on a new life.

Garret was very confident and self-assured about the urgency of his intervention. Not one of the women agreed with him. His message was: 'If these reforms have not come about it is because the system responds to pressure, all kinds of pressure, and there haven't been pressures in this area. There hasn't been pressure for civil rights from women.'

A very reasonable view, one would think, from someone in a position and of a mind to know. However his intervention turned the entire programme into a screaming match, a true *Late Late Show* circus. The production team must have loved it. The cause of much of the anger was that here we were at last articulating the dire situation of women in Ireland and a politician, who already had many platforms for his views, tried to steal the show and knock us off-course.

June Levine, who later became a researcher on the *Late Late*, summed up the programme in her book *Sisters*:

The show had been chaotic in spite of all the orchestration. Almost everything we had planned to avoid had happened. Mary Kenny had got shrill, the rest of us hadn't exactly kept our cool, the Marxists had taken up valuable time and a man had stolen the limelight.

Fortunately, our message penetrated through the chaos; for women all over the country it was the wake-up call they needed. The following month, when Women's Liberation organised a meeting in Dublin's Mansion House, more than a thousand women turned up. For hours that night women queued to give powerful testimony of the reality of their lives and to pledge support for the women's lobby.

Around this time, Senator Mary Robinson introduced a private member's family planning bill to amend the 1935 Criminal Law Amendment Act but it was sidelined in the Seanad. This bill resulted in the reading of a letter from the Archbishop of Dublin, Dr John Charles McQuaid, at all Sunday Masses in the diocese. Women's liberation organised a walk-out at Masses and that Sunday evening organised a picket on the Archbishop's residence in Drumcondra. Some women walked out of several Masses and Mary Kenny delivered a homily before she walked out of her local church. Although such actions were all very shocking and very untypical of Irish women in those days, public support for and solidarity with the stated objectives of Women's Liberation remained constant.

Support began to wane only in the aftermath of the 'contraceptive train' protest. This event was widely publicised just a month after the *Late Late Show*. On 22 May 1971, forty-seven women along with journalists and camera crews from BBC and NBC took a morning train to Belfast for the sole purpose of buying condoms, which were then illegal in the south of Ireland. Mary Kenny and Nell McCafferty were among the women on the shopping tour of Belfast pharmacies. The women's plan was to orchestrate a confrontation with customs officers on their return to Dublin's Connolly Station. Women would demand to be searched, expecting that when the contraband was found they would be arrested and charged.

The plan backfired, in so far as the Dublin customs officers ignored the flagrant provocation. No arrests were made and the chance to show the idiocy of the contraception laws was lost. It was all manna from heaven for the press corps and got raving headlines next day. I was not involved on this occasion, mainly because we had already planned a family holiday in Spain, but in truth I felt the stunt was too histrionic and had advised caution when the venture was discussed at meetings.

Inevitably there were adverse reactions. Betty Byrne, president of the thousand-member-strong Irish Federation of Women's Clubs, stated that it would be a pity if the Irish Women's Liberation Movement were to become identified in the public mind with ardent demonstrations on a few highly controversial issues. These women, she said 'were not typical'.

Commenting on her statement, an editorial in the *Irish Independent* asked: 'Is it [Irish Women's Liberation] to moderate its tone in a bid to capture the support of women like Mrs Byrne, an established leader in her own right, or is it to become a pioneering lobby for instant reform, the need for which is generally conceded but also generally regarded as better sought for stage by stage?'

After the contraceptive train, the group was more disorganised than ever and the deficiencies in structure and framework were compensated for with more bizarre protests. In support of Mary Robinson's contraceptive bill in the Seanad, four women protesting at Leinster House decided to climb in through a window, which brought them into the men's toilet. Inevitably women regarded these activities with dismay and many began distancing themselves from the movement.

Those still in the Women's Liberation group now decided that structure and planning was needed. But it was too late: the original group had fragmented; Mary Kenny was gone; splits had developed and many of us were exhausted and frustrated.

I resigned publicly in October 1971, disappointed by what I regarded as a lost opportunity for the women's cause. In hindsight, of course, I see that this was not the case. An important and irreversible start had been made to changing thinking. Irish Women's Liberation carved a courageous path, which many more conventional organisations followed. For me, being part of such a dynamic group and working with such motivated and idealistic women was a valuable experience. Although short-lived, the Irish Women's Liberation Movement had a profound effect on the Irish establishment and set in motion an unstoppable series of changes.

In truth a sober, sensible, structured organisation

would not have delivered the necessary jolt, would not have grabbed the headlines, would not have shocked men and women alike into an awareness of the inferior legal and social status of women. People may have disliked much of what Women's Liberation did but they could not ignore it. Women's Liberation was the breeding ground for many of the pressure groups that followed: AIM, Adapt, Irish Women's Aid, Cherish, FLAC, Gingerbread and Irish Women United. All of these were practical organisations with, in the main, dual objectives: to lobby government on women's rights and to give marginalised women practical help and support.

As I licked my wounds after Women's Liberation had fragmented, I decided that the road to equality would be longer than I thought. Little did any of us suspect then just how long and difficult it would be.

5

Starting Over

After the fragmentation of the Irish Women's Liberation Movement, media and public interest in women's issues waned. As far as commentators and editors were concerned, that circus had run its course. As the Northern Ireland conflict intensified, with the bombing of the Post Office Tower in London, internment in Northern Ireland and mass demonstrations in London and Dublin, the newspapers, radio and television reflected what was happening. We were living in a seriously difficult and uncertain time. There was little public appetite for women's issues, which by now were regarded as frivolous and largely as being the publicity-seeking activities of a small radical group.

The eventual demise of Irish Women's Liberation was inconclusive and unsatisfactory; many women felt let down, even puzzled at what we saw as self-destruction. How could critical social issues that had been relevant six months previously no longer seem to matter?

There had been no closure on the group and no forum for analysis or discussion about what had gone wrong or even about what future action was necessary. After all, in our short existence the critical need for reform had been proven. I certainly felt that the many problems that women had revealed at meetings and by letter illustrated a grave need for radical change. In my view, to do nothing would mean abandoning the women and the cause to a continuation of the status quo for the foreseeable future. Other colleagues felt the same. I received phone calls and letters asking me to continue the work we had been doing, to keep up the campaign.

I took time to ponder and to sort through the rubble of the break-up and of my very public resignation row. With hindsight I realised it was unacceptable to be so offensive in my resignation statement about other women also committed to the women's cause. Writing it, I was driven by frustration and a sense of my powerlessness to influence the trends and directions of Irish Women's Liberation. To colleagues my resignation smacked of pique and betrayal. In any event it left a legacy of bitterness, which I regret to say manifested itself in later years in some harsh media coverage I received when I was Minister of State for Women's Affairs. More than any other life experience up to then, my time in Women's Liberation politicised me and I know it clarified my priorities. (My letter of resignation appears as Appendix 1 in this book.)

Dana Davis, then editor of the largest-selling Irish women's magazine, *Women's Choice,* contacted me and was the catalyst I needed. Dana was utterly persuasive and convinced me to stay involved, pointing out that direct action for legislative change was the only option for real reforms. She had not been involved in Women's

Liberation, nor in any other organisation for that matter, but was a strong supporter of women's rights, for her own and everyone else's daughters. We met and agreed to see if we could continue the work in another forum, not at that time an easy proposition. Could or should we start all over again? Finding a blueprint was not going to be easy: what was needed, in effect, was to metamorphose Women's Liberation into another organisational form. With the plethora of disadvantages, inequalities and discriminations suffered by women now revealed, on what issues might the initial focus be?

To explore the possibilities, a small group of women met at my home in Foxrock in early 1971. This group included Dana Davis, Deirdre McDevitt, a friend from our schooldays, Madeleine Prendergast, Tessa Bond, Bernadette Quinn, a pharmacist, Máire Humphreys, a nurse, Joan O'Brien, a teacher, and Anne McAllister, a longtime neighbour and friend. They all came to find out what was happening and stayed. We all had young children, home responsibilities and some full-time or part-time work. We all agreed on the need for a new organisation for women and further meetings were planned which were attended by three husbands of members, the late Cathal McAllister, Peter Prendergast and Brian Fennell. In those early days we benefited greatly from the expertise and guidance of Peter Prendergast, who was then a marketing consultant. Later on I would have dealings with him in his role as general secretary of Fine Gael and government press secretary in the coalition government of 1983-7.

The ad hoc group took two firm decisions: there would be no precipitate publicity and whatever name we eventually decided for the organisation could not include the word 'woman' or 'women'. A majority view prevailed that we needed distance between us and the existing image of Women's Liberation as a publicity-seeking group. We also had to accept that women's rights in Ireland were very much children's rights as well. Fundamental issues like lack of contraception and divorce, lack of statutory rights to maintenance in marriage and unmarried pregnancy directly and indirectly affected the condition of children. Not being pigeonholed into the women's issues slot would be important, we felt, if we wanted our work to be taken seriously.

We decided to keep the group small and manageable. First we would conduct a thorough research of the Irish social and legal landscape as it applied to women. This meant women's role in marriage and the family. Only after compiling a report, quantifying the problems and identifying our aims and objectives would we go public with a launch. Interestingly enough we adopted the Women's Liberation non-hierarchical structure: meeting chairpersons rotated and work was allocated according to skills, experience and the time people had available. It seems a simple plan and it worked.

After carrying out research for almost a year the group, now called AIM (Action, Information and Motivation), decided to concentrate its efforts on influencing the introduction of legislation to give Irish women and children an enforceable legal right to a proportion of the family income. Our study had shown a pitiful state of family poverty when financial support by a husband was inadequate or withdrawn. In the European context, married women in Ireland were tolerating a punitive situation. Other European countries had either traditionally upheld a woman's right to fair maintenance in marriage or had introduced laws to give necessary protection. It is important to note that, unlike neighbouring countries, marriage at that time was the majority 'career' for Irish women, because the marriage bar prevailed, compelling women to leave their public service jobs when they got married. Marriage law in the early 1970s vested most rights in the husband. These included rights to the family home, family income, social welfare and even to children's allowance from the state.

Could a new breed of activist women change all this, most of us middle-class mothers in our thirties with no organisational or political experience or formal legal training? We decided, yes, we could, and we launched an intense political and legal campaign.

In my head I kept hearing Garret FitzGerald's rebuke on *The Late Late Show:* that women had never articulated their problems to political audiences. Would it be that simple? In our naïveté some of us honestly believed that change would come in two or three years. Surely the consequences to families of inadequate policies and legislation – as the AIM group was able to document – were so terrible that politicians would act quickly. But progress was much more sluggish: only minimal changes came after four years and the campaign lasted all of fifteen years.

Some founder members were asked to write about their memories of the early days of the group for the summer 1985 edition of *AIM Group Magazine.*

According to Bernadette Quinn:

Feelings among women had reached boiling point and this unified feeling of frustration was our catalyst to start the group. Of course there were the inevitable remarks – we were a crowd of middle-class do-gooders. But we sincerely believed that this should not stop us wanting to change an unjust situation, especially when the women most affected had no energy or power to change their lives.

For Pam Lynch:

At that time a battered wife had no legal right to defend herself against assault by her husband. Even if the police took him to court she was simply there in her capacity as their witness. When she got the right to apply for a barring order we felt a tremendous step had been taken in giving her some right to protect herself.

Anne McAllister remembers:

I had a baby in the middle of the first year and can remember rushing off to lobby politicians or attend a communications course, always arriving breathless and late. They were heady days and we were all absolutely committed.

How the women who wrote to us un-burdened themselves, despite the fact that we were complete strangers to them. I used to go home at night with my mind whirling in confusion, unable to sleep or think of anything else.

For Deirdre McDevitt:

One of my strongest memories will always be our first public meeting. Among the TDs there was a tendency to think we were going over the top, exaggerating the stories of injustices that we said were happening to women around the country. Then several women stood and told their personal histories and this created a true context. We heard afterwards that one TD had been unable to sleep that night!

During our year of research and planning other women joined the core group: Frances Dolan, Miriam Moore, Mary Higgins, Pam Lynch, Ursula Wheatley, Trudi Visser, Teresa Butterfield, Mary Banotti, the late Betty Gallagher and Anne Williams, Teresa Long, Isobel Butler, Valerie Curran, Mary O'Neill. All these women had children but somehow were also infected with a zeal to contribute whatever they could to the organisation. Some women stayed a year or two; others for ten years or more. Years later we meet and are still friends.

AIM Group was a new breed of women's organisation. Our time and activities were firmly focused on policies for women and children. We were involved in daily meetings, lobbying, legal and political workshops, counselling, fundraising, publicity and public speaking. In the early days we never took a break for summer or Christmas holidays, the times of greatest stress on families. AIM Group was a place for hard work and no one stayed if they just wanted to kill time or make social contacts. Nonetheless we did have fun and although the problems were grim at times and progress slow, we stuck together, kept our focus and kept our sense of humour.

In advance of our launch on 11 January 1972, AIM Group members studied the laws related to marriage and their application. We learned how the courts worked, secured all the relevant statistics referring to marriage breakdown and identified key departmental and political spokespersons. Where possible we identified specific members of the judiciary.

We spent a day understanding public relations and received media training in the Catholic Communications Centre. Father Tom Savage, then a priest in the Communication Institute, and now a director of the Communications Clinic and Chairman of the RTÉ Authority, was our tutor. This training was invaluable. It sharpened our awareness of the media and developed our broadcasting techniques.

Our formal launch as an organisation was held in Brian Fennell's office in 38 Clarendon Street, Dublin. The objectives of our platform were:

- enforceable maintenance in marriage
- equal rights to the family home
- attachment of earnings
- free legal aid

A large number of media people attended on the night, although newspaper coverage next day was disappointing. Under the heading of 'Twenty women form new organisation', *The Irish Times* gave us three paragraphs on 12 January. I felt that some journalists, who came expecting Women's Liberation Mark Two, saw otherwise and left us alone for then. And that suited us fine! In the following weeks we participated countrywide in radio and TV interviews and panel discussions. This, if we needed it, was our kick-start. We got an overwhelmingly positive response and confirmation that our platform was very relevant indeed.

The Fianna Fáil party was then in government: Desmond O'Malley TD was Minister for Justice and Jack Lynch TD was Taoiseach. Political focus at that time was on Ireland acceding as a full member of the European Economic Community (as the European Union was then called) the following year. A general election was due in 1973.

We regarded both these events as timely and to our advantage. We intended to extract agreements to legislative action from all parties in advance of the general election and to let them know that we would be around to ensure they would be delivered. This period, the early 1970s, was a critical time for Ireland's future. Profound changes would be occurring because of the necessity of complying with EEC practice and this would affect all our lives; yet women had no direct stake in the decision-making process and played no role in determining events. In those days only men were in the power towers of religion, law, business and politics. The role of Irish women was fixed in time and we had the spurious protection of Article 41 of the 1937 *Constitution of Ireland:*

> In particular the State recognises that by her life within the home, woman gives to the State a support without which the common good cannot be achieved.
>
> The State shall, therefore, endeavour to ensure that mothers shall not be obliged by economic necessity to engage in labour to the neglect of their duties in the home.

This image of women as passive and nurturing, along with the meaningless state 'responsibility' for them was then and still is repugnant to modern Irish women and Irish men. In my view this article should be removed. For many years it has reflected neither the spirit nor the reality of the life of Irish women.

As AIM Group spearheaded its marriage law reform campaign in 1972, the spotlight was being turned on other women in the margins: single mothers and widows. Over the years Irish society had adopted a punitive and judgemental attitude towards single mothers. These women were rejected at every level – family, community and employment – in a sort of national dread. They were often banished from their homes and jobs, hidden in convents or sent abroad. They could be dismissed from employment because of pregnancy. This shame and condemnation drove many women to a lonely existence in England. If they stayed in Ireland until their confinement, they were hidden away in mother and baby homes managed by religious orders, then obliged to give their babies up for adoption They were socially stigmatised and their children denied equality in law.

One young, unmarried women called Maura O'Dea became pregnant in 1970. She decided to keep her baby and to challenge attitudes to unmarried motherhood. In 1972, along with six other single mothers, she set up an organisation called Cherish. It was a lobby group but also a support and resource group for women and their babies and it played a significant role in the introduction of state maintenance, the Unmarried Mothers' Allowance, in 1973.

Gemma Rowley, a Dublin social worker, and Father Fergal O'Connor, a Dominican priest, launched another organisation for single mothers, Ally, in 1971. Ally provided family placements for pregnant girls until their confinement and introduced options other than having their babies adopted. Above all, like Cherish, it challenged and eventually changed public attitudes to Ireland's unmarried mothers.

Since 1967, widows had been organised by the dynamic Eileen Proctor in the National Association of Widows. Although widowhood was regarded as a respectable state and accepted by officialdom – and was certainly in a different category from single or deserted wives – life for many widows was grim and difficult. In the campaigning climate of the 1970s, widows too became more militant. To highlight their demands, the National Association of Widows held a meeting in Liberty Hall in November 1972 and created their own bit of history. For the first time ever, members took to the streets and marched from Liberty Hall to Dáil Éireann in support of change. Wonder of wonders: sensible widow women on Dublin streets with placards!

Two other women's organisations existed in 1972, both conservative in outlook and cautious on controversial issues. Founded in 1910, the Irish Countrywomen's Association (ICA) comprised mainly rural women. It was very well supported and played a major role in improving the lives and the livelihoods of farm women, through developing a country market network and life-skills education. The ICA leaders prided themselves on being 'non-political'; they depended on government subvention for their activities and towards the upkeep of their college in Termonfeckin, County Louth. They were deaf to all appeals to use their considerable muscle in support of women's rights. However they did help AIM Group's campaign and in later years developed a practical political thrust.

Another organisation dating from 1942 (until 1992), the Irish Housewives' Association, was identified as a consumer organisation, which campaigned at the start about food rationing, food prices and poverty. Founder member Hilda Tweedy was instrumental in focusing attention on Irish women's rights at the European Union, the Council of Europe and the United Nations. On many occasions, travelling at her own expense, she would have been the only Irish representative at numerous international fora on women's rights. Attic Press published Hilda Tweedy's story of the association, *A Link in the Chain*, in 1992.

It is interesting to note that in 1972 no group or organisation was campaigning for legalisation of contra-ception. Since the demise of Women's Liberation and the pill train débâcle, only one person had the motivation to tackle both the Catholic Church and the government, both of which institutions opposed change.

This notable exception was of course Senator Mary Robinson, who single-mindedly, with only a handful of political supporters and no hope of success, introduced a private member's bill in the Seanad to legalise contraception. In a Fianna-Fáil-dominated Seanad she saw her Health (Family Planning) (Amendment) Bill repeatedly failing to get a first reading. Describing these attempts in a Dáil debate on the Health (Family Planning) (Amendment) Bill, which eventually regularised the law on contraception in 1985, Fine Gael TD John Kelly, who was a senator in 1972, stated:

> One thing Mary Robinson tried to do week after weary week was to get on the floor of the house the question of birth control.
>
> Day after day she was literally trampled on by the Fianna Fáil majority led by Senator Tommy Mullins. I thought him a rogue, part of the reason I thought so was the brutal contempt with which he and the whole Fianna Fáil party in the Seanad treated Senator Robinson.

It is notable that John Kelly would not have been a supporter of Mary Robinson's bill: he was a radical conservative. Once, when pressed about his views at a Dublin South constituency meeting he asked; 'Why let the Fianna Fáil Party have the conservative majority?'

I was told that a senior Fine Gael senator would not even handle Mary Robinson's bill when speaking, for fear of contamination. Tommy Mullins was not a lone opponent: the entire Fianna Fáil Party, then in government, displayed only contempt for Mary Robinson's bill and sabotaged all efforts to make contraception legal and available.

Under the 1935 Criminal Law Amendment Act, the supply and sale of all contraceptives were prohibited, while the Censorship of Publications Acts 1929 and 1946 prohibited the publication of material that advocated the unnatural prevention of conception. Access to proper family planning was very difficult, health information was scant and any normal contraception that worked was associated with a sub-culture of illegality and sin. Some women were on the pill but it was tightly controlled, requiring a medical prescription as a 'cycle regulator'.

Catholicism was the religion practised by most couples. If you did not want to get pregnant, the rhythm method and coitus interruptus were the only options approved of by the Catholic Church. The rhythm method was practised, with sad consequences, it has to been said, for many couples. It was both unreliable and psychologically damaging.

The attitude of the Catholic hierarchy was absolutely against any change and their opposition bedevilled any political move to amend the law. It was then accepted practice for government ministers to consult with the relevant archbishop in advance of policy proposals which would put 'Irish public morality' at risk. Eventual legislative change came more as a result of the Northern

Ireland peace process than respect for the needs of women. It became clear that any future Council of Ireland would not accept the influence of the Catholic Church.

Only a few general practitioners would prescribe the pill and Catholic women who were on the pill had to confess this fact to a priest and seek absolution. It was not unusual for sympathetic doctors who prescribed the pill to be 'outed' by conservative colleagues or other commentators. Women who identified understanding and helpful general practitioners passed on the word to other women. Similarly there was a small network of understanding priests to whom to confess. A Dublin acquaintance of mine who was on the pill for years, travelled the three hundred and twenty-mile round trip every month to confess to a priest in Cork.

So it was in a climate of repression and suspicion that the AIM Group women began work. We went regularly to Leinster House to brief ministers and party spokespersons and combined this with a publicity campaign. No social support service existed then, so we established counselling and support networks for the hundreds of women who contacted us. But we knew we could not let our focus change from the political to the social. It would have been easy and understandable but there were firm and regular reminders that we were seeking long-term political goals.

Our ultimate plan was to harvest support countrywide for the legal reforms we identified and publicised. We embarked on a speaking circuit, visiting rural branches of the Irish Countrywomen's Association and other women's clubs and associations. After outlining our action plan, we asked each meeting to pass a resolution of support and send it to their local Dáil representatives and to the government and to publicise it locally. The momentum this created was extraordinary, both in terms of motivating people, of public awareness and above all of political pressure, which gradually had an impact on government.

Despite the fact that these meetings put a strain on our small number of members, involving overnights away, we covered every part of the country. On the home front I think I was fairly organised. None of my colleagues ever questioned the work they did: they sorted their children out first, arranged food and school clothes and took off. I don't recall having scruples about being away from Brian and the children so much – it was just something I needed to do. But without Brian's extraordinary understanding and support it would just not have been possible.

One positive outcome was the establishment of five local branches of AIM Group, including Cork, Limerick and Galway, which functioned independently but reported to and liaised on lobbying with the Dublin group. Other trade union and social work groups, lawyers and doctors became interested and were very supportive. But not everyone liked what we were saying. Whenever I spoke to meetings around Dublin, some self-appointed moral crusaders turned up to heckle and disrupt. One of them was a postmistress and mother of twelve, Mena Uí Cribín, who would hurl allegations, accusing AIM Group of being pro-abortionists, family wreckers and anti-Catholic Church. At the time there was an organisation called Mná na hÉireann, to which Mena Uí Cribín and her colleagues belonged. Dealing with Mena was easy if she was alone: I listened and countered her claims and usually the women present took up the challenge. What was not so agreeable was when she came with supporters who had the potential to wreck the meeting.

Often our single-issue campaign appeared unsustainable. We were confronted almost daily by needs for other reforms. Many families were bigger than parents could cope with or afford, so should AIM Group not be working for contraception? Some marriages were beyond saving, so what about a divorce campaign?

These were valid questions, which we spent many evenings debating. In 1973 we seemed to be living in a hypocritical country, where powerful self-appointed moral guardians protected so-called Irish 'family values'. While divorce and contraception were seen as 'sexier' issues, more high-profile in the media than the activities of AIM Group, we just did not have the confidence that either public opinion or political will was ready to change the status quo. We had become sufficiently politically astute to know that more time and greater persuasion were needed for both contraception and divorce but we knew that other changes were possible in the short term, and we were determined not to be diverted from AIM Group's agenda.

While nobody, not even the Catholic hierarchy, could argue against reform in the area of family support, both contraception and divorce were contentious and divisive. As a group we had no ideological problem with contraception or divorce. AIM Group supported those platforms: we just did not want to dilute our principal objective. We were practical women; we wanted the time and energy we spent on our campaign to translate into concrete reforms that would make a difference to women's lives.

The Irish Constitution of 1937 prohibited legislation for divorce, so the hands of Irish parliamentarians were tied. The national referenda on the Constitution and legislation to alter this were still twenty-five years away from where we were in 1972. When marriages broke up and couples separated, inadequate legal remedies existed and remarriage was not possible for either party, unless, that is, one party succeeded in securing either a state or a church annulment. The first facilitated a second legal marriage but illegitimised the children of the first union, while the second facilitated a Catholic church wedding but not a second legal marriage recognised by the State. Both these remedies put children of the marriage at a disadvantage but although they were far from ideal, people availed of them as the only options.

There were other escapes from marriage – but only for a husband. A separated or deserting husband could leave the country, establish his domicile outside Ireland, divorce his Irish wife from that domicile and remarry. Irish law recognised these divorces, although it had no role in determining maintenance, property or other rights for the wives involved. Under Irish law married women then had dependent domicile (the same domicile as their husbands). This could result in their being divorced in a foreign jurisdiction with neither warning nor consultation, despite the Irish constitutional ban on divorce and despite the fact that they lived in Ireland.

Such Irish solutions to Irish problems were all too common. This concept of dependent domicile was offensive to women. I had the job and the joy, as Minister for State, of enacting the Domicile and Recognition of Foreign Divorces Act 1986, which ended this discrimination.

Within a year AIM Group had attained a serious and respectable public profile and because 1973 was a general election year it made an impact on all the political parties. That election resulted in a Coalition government of the Fine Gael and Labour parties, headed respectively by Taoiseach Liam Cosgrave TD and Tánaiste Brendan Corish TD.

In an AIM Group newsletter in June 1973 we reported that the new Minister for Social Welfare, Frank Cluskey TD, stated that he intended to make the children's allowance payable to mothers and to reduce the waiting time for deserted wives' allowance from six to three months. It was our first breakthrough – someone was listening after all! It was a promising start to the delivery of our agenda. The new Minister for Justice, Paddy Cooney TD, and Attorney General, Declan Costello, had a meeting with AIM Group and gave undertakings to introduce free legal aid and family maintenance reform. These were small advances in words, not actions, but this was how our campaign succeeded and our objectives were achieved.

It has to be said that Paddy Cooney has not got enough credit for his role in introducing family law legislation in the mid-1970s. His first piece of legislation was the Maintenance Orders Act of 1974, to allow maintenance orders and attachment of earnings against spouses working in the United Kingdom. This was followed by the Family Law (Maintenance of Spouses and Children) Act 1976 which gave relief for non-maintained families. Most importantly, it instituted judicial barring orders for violent husbands. Later on came the Family Home Protection Act 1976, which prevented the sale of the family home if both spouses did not consent. This body of law constituted a substantial advance in basic rights in marriage for women and vindicated AIM Group's years of campaigning. Encouraged by the achievement of our basic objectives, we realised that our work had to continue – to see the legislation enforced, to monitor cases when they came to court and generally keep an eye on the implementation of the new, complex legislation.

We realised that the women and children involved had been in the shadows for too long and had suffered social, financial and legal discrimination. We also realised that any diversion to meet the needs of this group would weaken AIM Group's central political thrust. But we had to do something. We formed a sister group for deserted people, both women and men. In April 1973 ADAPT (Association for Deserted and Alone Parents) was born. As a support group it helped to relieve the loneliness and isolation of alone parenthood; it put people in touch and gave information and expert help where needed. Suddenly the status of 'deserted' became a badge of identity, of a right to fight for legal rights, an invitation to move out of the shade.

Such was ADAPT's success and relevance that several countrywide branches sprang up. A Danish woman, the late Agnethe Grey, who lived in Dundalk, gathered local support and opened an ADAPT centre in the town, only to discover a huge need for the association's support. The success of ADAPT was in large part due to the dynamism of a new team of voluntary organisers. Its visibility ended the closet culture for many women who had previously been forced by Irish society to hide when they were deserted by their husbands. Many endured lives of desperation, as did their children. Some of there stories are recorded in a book I wrote which was published in 1974, called *Irish Marriage How Are You!* We got letters telling of situations that were hard to credit but they were all verified.

Such a case was that of Mary from Cavan who went to live with her widowed mother-in-law when she married. She and her husband had three children. When her husband left and went to Britain, Mary, who had no relatives or independent income, remained beholden to her husband's mother. She was little better than a slave in the home, doing farmwork and housework in order to keep a roof over her children's heads. We visited Mary and gave her advice and hope and she eventually came to Dublin and made a new home.

By 1974 it was obvious to many of us that we were not seeing the entire picture of Irish marriage and that there was another pressing problem: family violence. Some members of the group felt a growing unease at the level of what was then called 'wife-beating' with which we were being confronted. This was before barring or protection orders came in and assault cases were heard in open court, where a wife's 'alleged' injuries could be exhibited. The husband invariably had a solicitor but often the wife did not. The following day's newspapers would publish details of the cases. The outcome was usually a fine or a suspended sentence. This left the family intact and the husband still in the home, and inevitably meant further violence against a wife who no longer had confidence in the courts.

Those wives who went to court never received justice. They had neither financial means nor property rights, they did not qualify for legal aid, and the presiding judges were middle-class men who showed poor understanding of the life and needs of married women.

By my reckoning this problem of family violence was much worse that desertion. Real pain and suffering were being inflicted and children were being psychologically damaged. Battered wives were very much on their own. People would not interfere when the row was behind the hall door. The Gardaí were reluctant to take action and only did so in crisis situations.

While acknowledging the existence of this violence, my colleagues in AIM Group felt that our work would produce legislation that would of itself resolve the problem and that AIM should not get directly involved. I respected that decision but was still nagged by the need to do something, so I left the group for a year in early 1974 and went solo on dealing with family violence.

Two events brought matters to a head fairly rapidly. Firstly I got a phone call from a Father Ralph, a Garda chaplain in Mount Argus (a Passionist monastery and church in Kimmage in Dublin), seeking help with accommodation for a mother and six small children. The mother had been hospitalised the previous night, having been thrown down the stairs by her husband (a Garda), while the children were divided among neighbours. Now the mother was about to be discharged. It was not safe for mother and children to return to the family home but they needed to be together. Accommodation was the difficulty. Could I suggest a solution?

None of the ten residential facilities for the homeless that I phoned would take the entire family: some could take the children, or the baby; others the mother alone. To separate the members of the family would only compound the abuse they had already suffered. Just as my husband Brian and I felt we had drawn a blank on hostels and had decided to book them all in to the Montrose Hotel in Stillorgan, to give us thinking space, a message came that accommodation was available in a convent and retreat centre in Dún Laoghaire. There the family stayed safely for three weeks.

Soon after this something else happened that went to the heart of the problem. A BBC *Panorama* documentary called *Scream Quietly or the Neighbours Will Hear*, about Erin Pizzey and her work in the Chiswick Women's Aid Centre in London, was broadcast in Ireland. Two Irish mothers spoke of the lack of protection against their violent Irish husbands. They said that the UK hostel was the only safe option available for mothers like themselves and their children. I was sad and angry that Irish women were so helpless, so totally vulnerable. What about the constitutional recognition of women's role in the home? These cases of Irish domestic violence were a manifestation of the problems AIM Group was single-handedly trying to resolve.

When the programme ended at midnight, I wrote a letter to *The Irish Times* commenting on the programme, which was published on 1 March 1974. I received an overwhelming response from ordinary people and professionals alike and it was clear that I had touched a nerve. Many people were concerned about domestic violence and wanted to do something about it.

In mid-March I organised a public meeting in Buswell's Hotel in Dublin and as usual a committee was formed. It included Mary Banotti, later MEP for Dublin, Jane Tottenham, Muireann Wilson, Susan Donnelly, Cecily Golden, Mary Gormley, Sasha Kenny, David Murphy and Brian Fennell. Decisions were taken very quickly. We decided we would take a cue from Erin Pizzey and call the organisation Irish Women's Aid. Mary Banotti, Susan Donnelly and I visited Chiswick Hostel in London and met Erin Pizzey, as well as a number of Irish mothers. They told us that fear for themselves and their children had driven then to Chiswick, where they were welcomed and supported. We realised the enormity and complexity of the task ahead. One thing was clear: providing a shelter for families would require a great deal of money.

Erin Pizzey explained that she could tap into numerous UK charitable trusts for capital spending whereas at that time, funding for most social causes in Ireland had to be sourced on a voluntary basis and was a slow, tedious graft of organising functions and begging from friends and acquaintances. Needless to say a social cause, which involved (as it was perceived then) breaking up families would not exactly be a popular one. In those days few wished to open the Pandora's box of the problem Irish family. On the one hand, the family was an institution recognised by our Constitution while on the other it was forsaken by the laws and institutions of the state.

To help us to get established Erin Pizzey came to Dublin in May 1974 and appeared as a guest on *The Late Late Show*. In those days she was a large and formidable woman, who wore brightly coloured clothes; she was extremely self-confident and authoritative and had an infectious sense of humour. She was responsible for putting the problem of family violence on the political agenda in the UK. She was unequivocal about the needs of battered wives and took no prisoners. She was a skilled communicator and the Irish public responded generously to her television appeal, with offers of money, clothes and furniture.

The hostel venture began to take shape the week after the programme, when businessman Joe McMenamin rang and offered to lend us a big old house in Harcourt Street in Dublin, which was situated beside the Four Provinces Ballroom and near the Garda station. With a shelter so close to the city we thought our problems were solved. Unbelievably, there were no strings attached to the house loan. The fact that the house was old, shabby, cold and draughty did not deter us. It was central and could be made secure for families.

This house became a focus of intense activity. Frank Crummey, then a social worker with the ISPCC, got a truck and collected old furniture. Nora Owen, who was later a TD and Minister for Justice, appeared, always eminently practical, with her own bucket and scrubbing brush. Child psychiatrist Paul McQuaid offered to work with the children, as did the late actor John Molloy. The kindness and generosity of the public were overwhelming. Committee members of Irish Women's Aid metamorphosed into cooks, child-carers, cleaners and DIY experts. Even before repair work was completed, families moved in. I am not sure how we escaped prosecution, or being closed down, because we broke every rule in the planning and fire safety book.

Within weeks there were fifty women and children taking refuge from serious violence. After one very abusive and angry husband smashed his way into the house, beat up his wife and traumatised everyone, members of the committee had to take turns sleeping in as, due to lack of funds, paid staff was out of the question. On two other occasions husbands phoned members of the committee, instructing us to confiscate their wives' contraceptive pills while they were with us! On nights I slept in Harcourt Street, I questioned the usefulness of my role. I could not fend off an angry husband, neither was I a chaperone for the women, but as I slept in a room off the hall, door security was my priority. It certainly made for a poor night's sleep. Brian was a little anxious but went along with the arrangement.

Eventually a house-mother, Irish-American Barbara Horgan, was recruited at a salary of £100 a month. Like us, she had no experience in social care or organisation; we were all amateurs doing our limited best. As we accommodated an army of forty children, (the average family had five children) and many of the boys were wild and aggressive, things often got out of hand. On one occasion the boys dug a hole through the wall adjoining the next-door nurses' home and on another, used jars of donated baby food as missiles and painted the back wall of the house with puréed carrot. We moved the boxes of donated food out of their reach but had to deal with a solicitor's letter claiming damages for repair to the wall.

By early 1975, the hostel appeared to be functioning adequately. The women were getting social welfare payments and legal aid and the children were enrolled in local schools. Something had to be done to try and help the husbands of residents of the hostel. Father Chris Crowley of nearby Whitefriar Street Church, along with Brian Fennell, established a husband's support group and invited the men to come and talk. But it was a short-lived initiative because none of the husbands would openly discuss their violence, so strong was their conviction of their right to dominate their wives. The group was wound up but the efforts of the men to control the women continued.

In the early days, Irish Women's Aid had straight-forward expectations: to give protection to women and children; to win official recognition of the need for refuges to accommodate and care for abused families; and to reform the law. But as a consequences of the actions of the organisation, other changes occurred. The attitude of welfare officers and of court personnel to beaten women came under more public scrutiny. Bullying men realised that the balance of power in their relationships was changing because their wives now had advocates and options, inadequate as they appeared. Victims of domestic violence began to speak out: they became visible as they emerged from every parish and neighbourhood.

Many of the women in our hostel never returned to their husbands. Some benefited from the generosity of Dublin businessmen like Tony Byrne and the late Jack Curran, who loaned us small, second-stage homes which enabled the women to start new lives. Other women left the hostel after a few nights' respite but more often they determined, having taken the decision to leave the family home, to try to get their lives in order. At best that involved a sequence of changes, in order to get accommodation, legal protection and money. Nothing was straightforward or simple: the women and children had few entitlements and many needs. In many instances the option of returning to the family home, albeit to a potentially violent husband, seemed simpler than battling officialdom and the courts.

As the Irish Women's Aid campaign progressed, the workload became more complicated and difficult. We never had respite to carry out repairs or renovations to the house: it was always overcrowded because no woman in need was turned away as we tried to provide comprehensive help to the families, all with differing needs. In reality we found it difficult to cope and on some occasions took risks.

Theresa was a mother of five to whom we had been giving care and support. Two of her children were with her husband, a violent man living in Cork, two were with her and the youngest, a girl, had been sent over to a relative in the UK, whose address Theresa did not know. Her eight-year year old son, who was living with his father and sister in Cork, wrote her a letter which related that he had sharpened a knife to kill his father and that he kept it under his mattress. She appealed to us to help her to rescue her children. The correct help was legal action but Theresa felt that this would take too long. We agreed to drive her to her home village. I must emphasise that this was not the decision of the organisation, but of individuals responding to what we saw as a serious issue. Brian was the driver but I did not go along. Another woman from the organisation accompanied Theresa. Their intention was very clear: they would try to bring both the girl and boy back to Dublin. When they got there, the boy was playing on the road and he saw his mother and jumped into the car, but not before his father realised what was happening. With a roar the father started running, reached the car, grabbed the driver around the neck and held on. Brian kept driving, the man let go, and all four got back to Dublin safely. Theresa and her daughter were later reunited.

The risks involved in such an action do not bear thinking about. Within an hour, two local Gardaí were at our door, investigating a kidnapping. Theresa told them the full story and produced proof of identity and court papers and they left, satisfied. It seemed that at that time parents could not kidnap their own child: we had just facilitated the transport.

Things were slowly improving in the area of domestic violence. In some instances official agencies linked up to provide services that we could not afford: for instance, the health board and Dublin Corporation lent us a large suburban house with a garden to act as second-stage accommodation. But the fact remained that we were only a small voluntary group of ordinary people, confronting substantial social problems that should rightly have been the responsibility of the state. Having set up the first hostel and having confirmed the necessity for it, we would have been happy if it had been sponsored and further developed by state agencies. Above all we wanted to avoid a premature exit by the voluntary group and the subsequent collapse of the hostel.

The hostel survived for a number of years on a voluntary basis, moving location as more spacious accommodation was provided. Many concerned and dedicated people kept the service alive. It was not until years later that official agencies recognised the problems created by domestic violence and funded Irish Women's Aid and it was not until 1984, when Barry Desmond TD was Minister for Health in the 1983-7 coalition in which I served, that the first custom-built refuge was opened in Rathmines, Dublin.

I left the organisation after a year, along with some other founder members, totally exhausted. Other valiant volunteers continued the work of providing refuge for victims of domestic violence in a larger hostel. By then, Liz McManus (a Labour TD) had opened a small refuge in Bray, County Wicklow, and writer Maeve Kelly opened a refuge in Limerick. Gradually, state agencies woke up to the reality of marital breakdown in Irish society. The courts, the Gardaí, the Catholic Church and the social welfare network could no longer wash their hands of family violence.

6

My DIY General Election

The first ever general election I contested was in 1977 and it was as an independent candidate. It was one of my spontaneous leaps into the unknown and not really the recommended route into elected politics. I felt that the circumstances in 1977 left me with no other option. The Taoiseach Liam Cosgrave TD called a general election on 25 May with polling on 16 June, and there was a ripple of expectation among members of the Women's Political Association (WPA), which had been founded in 1971 to encourage women's participation in politics, and other politically-motivated women in all constituencies. The founders of the WPA were women like Gemma Hussey, Hilary Pratt and Phil Moore, and I joined the association at an early stage.

We felt sure that this would be the election to achieve a breakthrough for aspiring women in all the political parties. The number of women in the Oireachtas was very low. Of the 147 seats in the outgoing Dáil, only four were held by women deputies. Promoting the concept of equal political representation for women was then (and still is) a worthy end in itself. In the 1970s it was vital, given the inferior legal status of Irish women. The case for change did not appear to be a priority on the mainstream political agenda.

The Women's Political Association had devoted six years to public education and research with the aim of increasing women's participation in politics. Its focus was women and its aim to wake them up to the grave gender imbalance in politics. The WPA also targeted the party leaderships to encourage more positive approaches to promoting women at selection conventions.

In advance of the 1977 general election, the WPA polled all politicians to seek their commitment to legislative reforms for women if they were re-elected. The findings of this poll were released to the media. Jack Lynch, leader of Fianna Fáil, which was then in opposition, gave a positive response but both the Fine Gael and Labour parties (the outgoing coalition government) maintained a cool and reserved stance. Until, that is, media coverage indicated wide public support for the WPA position, which resulted in pre-election promises arriving fast and furious from all parties. Legal aid! Income tax reform! Family courts! It seemed that all would be realised whichever party won the election.

In reality paradise for women was not that near. Nothing changed in the promotion and selection of party candidates. For the political parties it was business as usual, as convention after convention chose male candidates. Out of 375 party candidates selected, only twelve were women. There were quiet screams of desperation from keen political women in the ranks of all parties. I certainly had little faith in promises of a future

Nuala's parents, Patrick and Elizabeth Campbell.

From left: Jacqueline, Amanda and Garrett Fennell, 1970.

An early AIM group meeting in Blackrock. From left: Deirdre McDevitt, Nuala Fennell, Ann McAllister, Tessa Bond, Cathal McAllister and Frances Dolan

On the lawn at Leinster House, 21 June 1981. From left: TDs Eileen Lemass, Ma Harney, Nora Owen, Mary Flaherty, Nuala Fennell and Alice Glenn.
(Photo: Sunday Tribune*)*

Nuala's first day in Dáil Éireann, Leinster House, 11 June 1981.
From left: Nuala's mother, Elizabeth Campbell, Nuala,
Amanda Fennell (aged thirteen) and Garrett Fennell (aged sixteen).

Nuala and Fine Gael Dublin South constituency chairman,
Kevin Norton (son of former Labour leader William Norton), February 1981.

Nuala with An tUachtarán, Dr Patrick Hillery, 1982.

From left: Mamo McDonald, Minister of State Nuala Fennell,
An Taoiseach Dr Garret FitzGerald TD, Sylvia Meehan (1985).

'Women in Irish Society' conference at the Catholic University of America, Washington DC, 11 April 1986. Senator Mary Robinson is third from the left and Nuala Fennell is on her left.

Nuala with Maura Wall Murphy of the Family Mediation Service, 1986.

*Rose of Tralee Brenda Hyland is one of the new Gardaí
at the passing-out ceremony in Templemore, 1986.*

Nuala at her 50th Birthday party, given by constituency officers, November 1985.

Nuala and Brian at the top of Ehrwalder Alm in Austria, January 1995.

Fine Gael political women photographed at Leinster House, December 2008.
From left: Gemma Hussey, Nuala Fennell, Mary Flaherty, Nora Owen,
Madeleine Taylor-Quinn, Monica Barnes and Myra Barry.

Nuala with (from left) Jacqueline, Garrett and Amanda Fennell, 1982.

Nuala and Brian with their grandchildren, Christmas 2007. From left: Eveline Hall, Amélie Gibbons, Kate Fennell, Ian Hall and James Fennell.

equality agenda by the political parties when I saw how easily the campaign for women candidates was ignored. Six years of consciousness-raising, lobbying party leaders and supporting prospective women candidates seemed to have missed the target.

In hindsight I feel that women may have been rather naïve in believing that destroying the male political monolith could be so simple. We were working with inadequate experience from inside the political process and did not appreciate the fierce competition for nominations, the extensive male networks and the vested interests. According to traditional criteria, women as candidates were not perceived as an electoral asset by party hierarchies unless they were widows, daughters, or granddaughters of former Oireachtas members.

Colleagues in WPA were deeply disappointed and frustrated by this turn of events but I had the sort of anger that wanted to do something about it and now! But what?

The last weekend of May in 1977 was gloriously sunny and Mary Banotti and I, along with our small daughters, were staying in Mary's cottage in Ardglassan, County Meath. We bought the *Sunday Press* and scrutinised the lists of declared candidates in all the constituencies. We decided over coffee that there had to be other ways of becoming a election candidate than being anointed by a political party. 'I'll do it, I'll go independent!' I announced. I put my small daughter Amanda into the car and drove back to Dublin to tell Brian. He, as usual, was not surprised.

Earlier in the year a group of friends had asked me to

put my name forward as an independent candidate on a women's ticket and although I was tempted I declined for certain family reasons. But on that May Sunday it was clear to me that if I felt deeply about what was happening, I had no option but to become a candidate. If women were ever to reach the goal of substantial political representation, we had to help ourselves in practical ways. For now, I would forget the gentle persuasion and well-mannered approach: there were other ways to change minds. Why not compete and challenge the system and in the process remove the mystique surrounding women's selection for election campaigns?

The closest I had been to Dáil Éireann was writing a budget as 'Minister for Finance' in the Irish Housewives' Association Model Parliament Conference. Deciding to run for election just two weeks before polling day made for a daunting campaign and was regarded by some as being a little mad. Writing and commenting on politics as a journalist was quite different from participating at the sharp edge of practical politics. My last-minute decision to stand was welcomed by most women and warmly supported by the Women's Political Association but greeted with scepticism by many politicians. Some political journalists bet that I would loose my £100 deposit.

If at the start of the week I had no money, no team, no literature or posters, by the end of it all of these had materialised. Money flooded in. One woman sent £150, a small fortune in 1977, and amongst the party women who supported me was Mary O'Rourke, then a Fianna Fáil councillor who had failed to get a nomination in

County Westmeath. She sent £25. My total election budget was £650.

I opted for Dublin South County constituency instead of Dún Laoghaire, where I then lived, because the late Una O'Higgins-O'Malley was standing in Dún Laoghaire on a peace and reconciliation ticket. She was the daughter of former Minister for Justice Kevin O'Higgins, who was assassinated by the IRA in 1927, when she was a baby. Una had a high profile and was a good and serious candidate. Unlike me she would not be a 'woman's' candidate, seeking what we then termed the 'women's vote', but nonetheless she was being supported by the WPA and by other women's organisations.

How did we define the 'women's vote'? Our belief was that women voters would vote across party lines for a worthy woman candidate, given our system of the single transferable vote. Voters could give a woman candidate their Number 1 or a high preference and continue preferences for their party choice. In my case this was what women voters did. Dublin South County was then a three-seat constituency and there were eight male candidates, among whom were the late Niall Andrews (Fianna Fáil), the late Ruairí Brugha (Fianna Fáil), Sean Barrett (Fine Gael), the late John Kelly (Fine Gael) and John Horgan (Labour).

Some feminists regarded what I was doing as a dangerous gamble but it seemed the only way to emphasise the need for real electoral choice, of gender as well as party, in future elections. I reckoned we didn't have the luxury of waiting another four years to prove our point. Thanks to the considerable energy and drive of WPA women Audrey Conlon, Phil Moore, Mavis Arnold, Hilary Pratt, Doreen Dalton and Gemma Hussey (who was running for a NUI seat in the Seanad), my campaign took shape. My twelve-year old son Garrett dealt with immediate priorities such as registration, compiling a voters' register and a constituency map. Garrett plotted and organised his way to the polling day while he was on his school holidays. He commandeered our house phone to organise meetings, delegated jobs, set up canvass teams and ordered stationery. Few realised that my acting director of elections was not yet a teenager.

As the information gaps disappeared and I developed a strategy for the weeks ahead, I began to feel more confident and less of a novice. The national campaign, spearheaded by the WPA, was remarkably professional and was intended to benefit independent candidates like me and, where local ground rules allowed, party women also. The WPA prepared a guide for women voters, ran a publicity campaign and organised a women helpers' network.

Almost all the women's organisations encouraged members to be selective with their votes and asked their members to support women candidates. Lapel and car stickers bearing the powerful slogan, 'Why Not a Woman?' were widely distributed and visible during the campaign.

My main objective was getting to front doors, to schoolyards and to shopping centres. The constituency stretched across Dublin South from the Dodder River to Bray and as far as the Dublin Mountains and the electorate numbered 48,000. As the calls and letters flooded in, we

organised huge teams of canvassers, morning, afternoon
and evening. Due to the limited time available I could
not cover the entire constituency. Garrett colour-coded
crucial areas on the constituency map to be canvassed on
my behalf. My friends in AIM Group, family members,
neighbours and friends all walked the pavements for two
weeks. It was the start of a political canvassing career for
many of the women, such as the late Betty Gallagher,
Trudy Visser, Isobel Butler, my sister Bernie and my
seventy-year-old mother-in-law, the late Effie Fennell.
Most of these women turned out for subsequent general
elections. The campaign became a magnet for women.
A valve of energy and creativity opened and pent-up
frustrations were released in a practical and positive way.

While she was canvassing in Ballinteer, a journalist
friend, the late June Levine, met a young mother who
was seriously hassled because her son's birthday cake
had come out of the oven as flat as a stone. June was a
renowned cook and she describes in *Sisters* how she rolled
up her sleeves and produced another cake – the quid pro
quo being a promise of a Number 1 vote. At this point
she was redeployed and cooked her way through the
campaign. The vote June earned was possibly offset the
next night when another campaigner, Nell McCafferty,
swore robustly when a voter's small dog jumped up and
bit her.

On the family front things were not so harmonious for
me. I hadn't really expected help or encouragement from
my parents for the campaign but neither did I expect the
ostracism that resulted. My mother and particularly my
father were ardent Fine Gael supporters and rejected the

independent line I had taken. My mother told me that it would be better if I neither phoned nor called to the house until the election was over because my father was so distressed at what I was doing. This could have upset me but it didn't. I understood their position and knew it was too late to convert them to the feminist cause.

Alongside an army of women doing everything from driving to babysitting, many men helped both on the canvass and in the background. Psychiatrist Ivor Browne volunteered to erect posters and, standing at six-foot-plus, he had no need for a ladder when securing posters to poles. Unlike other candidates, who had colour posters, we could only afford black and white posters. The newspapers and RTÉ gave good coverage to women candidates during the election campaign and to women and family issues where they existed in party manifestos.

The emphasis on women candidates and women's votes in the 1977 election pushed the issues of contraception, equal pay and divorce on to virtually every forum. Prior to the election, women had highlighted the critical need for legislative changes – but with little success. In the 1977 campaign, we watched party spokesmen squirm as they attempted to justify their past disregard for equality issues. However, they did not make worthwhile commitments for the future.

In relation to contraception there was uncertainty about the law as a result of the McGee case. In 1973, Mrs Mary McGee, a young mother, ordered contraceptives from a UK mail-order firm. The contraceptives were seized by customs. Mrs McGee challenged this decision by customs all the way to the Supreme Court. There, by a majority of four to one, the judges ruled in her favour. The Supreme Court recognised the existence of a constitutional right to marital privacy and ruled in her favour to import contraceptives for her own use, but so far the government had been unwilling to grasp the nettle of legislative change.

Charles Haughey TD (Fianna Fáil's spokesman on Health) spoke about contraception during the 1977 campaign and said, as reported in the *Irish Independent* of 27 May 1977, that he would have 'talks with a broad spectrum, including the Catholic Church'. Fianna Fáil party leader, Jack Lynch TD, was even more ambivalent. He stated that, following the McGee decision, contraceptives were too freely available and that the party favoured control at national level.

Predictably, with only two weeks to canvass voters, all Dublin South Constituency was not visited but certainly by polling day, our presence would have been felt in most of the homes. By election day, 16 June, our job was complete.

Under our system of proportional representation Irish election counts are a riveting spectator sport. From nine o'clock on the day of the count queues form outside the count centres, people seeking tickets to witness the progress of the count and learn the fate of the candidates and the parties. Usually tickets are reserved for party officials, candidates, workers and accredited journalists.

Never before having been to an election count, I was totally blasé, in contrast to my subsequent election counts which I approached with white-knuckle tension. At midday on 17 June 1977, when I walked into the count in the old Kilmacud National School, I knew we had made a difference. We had both lost and won. Though it was my first time at a count I had to pretend that I knew the procedure. It was like a séance, with men whispering in corners, others looking dark and anxious. Some stood at a barrier jotting hieroglyphs on sheets of paper as people inside the barrier unfolded the voting papers. Eventually the furtive glances in my direction became so pronounced that I had to ask what was happening. 'God, girl, you're doing grand,' one Fianna Fáiler told me. The outcome was that I got 10.25 per cent of the first preference votes, 3,828 lovely votes, and was not eliminated until the fourth count. My transfers were spread right across the parties but most of them helped to elect Labour's John Horgan.

It was never realistic for me to win a seat in 1977 and the achievement of a respectable vote was as much as I could hope. The sceptical journalists lost their money and I got back my deposit, which at the time was sufficient to fund a party for all those involved in the campaign.

So how did women fare? Six women were returned to the 147-seat Dáil, only one more than in the previous Dáil. They were Kit Ahern, Sile de Valera, Eileen Lemass and Máire Geoghegan-Quinn for Fianna Fáil, Joan Burke for Fine Gael and Eileen Desmond for Labour. In 1977 the 'dynasty' vote prevailed – three of the women were widows, one a daughter and one a granddaughter of former deputies. This is not to take away from the women, all of whom were competent politicians. When we looked at the first-preference votes cast for women in 1977, we were pleased to see that they had almost doubled to 81,967 from 42,268 in the previous election.

Three women were elected to the new Seanad: independents Gemma Hussey and Mary Robinson and Fianna Fáil's Tras Honan. Every new Taoiseach has nominating rights in the Seanad and Taoiseach Jack Lynch surprised everyone by appointing three women: Valerie Goulding, an activist for the handicapped, Mary Harney of Fianna Fáil and Eileen Cassidy of the Irish Countrywomen's Association.

For candidates every election campaign is different, but for pure excitement, vitality and fun, the campaign of 1977 stood out for me. Women made up the canvass and planning teams. Some belonged to groups and organisations, others did not, and like myself they had not been previously involved in politics. I think it was a turning point for the family too. We had all discovered new skills during the campaign. I had certainly got the political bit between my teeth, while Brian became resolved that I should pursue a political career. As always he was positive and supportive. After the election I re-established normal relations with my parents.

While the hard work of the WPA was not rewarded with a greater number of women winning seats in 1977, we saw proof that women could be an electoral asset. The campaign had also been a valuable learning experience and would stand political women in good stead for the future. I wrote about the campaign for the February 1978 issue if *Image* magazine:

> They [women] learned a great deal, like that being female is not in itself a deterrent to success but certainly means no grace and

favour treatment either.

They learned that male politicians would not willingly share their power space with women. They learned the limits to which men will go to sabotage female competition both at selection and election times…Rules are already made by men and once you know them you either play the game according to plan, or if they don't suit you, you think of ways to circumvent or change them.

In the same article, I noted the views Garret FitzGerald expressed at a WPA seminar in December 1977: 'Women's rights are the wrong reason to want to get into government. It may be a worthy motivation but it is not an acceptable political one.' I am not sure how this equates with his exhortation to us on the Women's Liberation *Late Late Show* to lobby politically for women's issues.

In the heady days of 1977 few women would have agreed with him. The cause of women's rights and women's equality were the engines that drove us because we had little reason to trust that male politicians would implement reforms for women. The passivity of Irish women up to then had enabled crucial issues like equal pay, contraception and property rights to be pushed to the level of the lowest political priority. In reality the general election of 1977 was the shot in the arm women needed. It generated determination and enthusiasm for women's own agenda in the electoral battles ahead.

7

Party Politics – Running for Europe and Dáil Éireann

Until I joined Fine Gael in 1978, I had had little interest in party politics and little confidence that any government could deliver the legislative change demanded by women's organisations. For many years the Women's Political Association had been encouraging women to become involved in politics. The message was: join parties, serve on committees, get involved in party organisation and seek nominations for local and general elections. As branches of WPA were formed countrywide, women responded in some numbers and began to challenge the political status quo on a local level.

My first contact with Fine Gael was in 1973 when, at the recommendation of the WPA, that we 'get involved' with a party, I attended a Fine Gael branch meeting in Blackrock, County Dublin. I could feel the shock waves from the assembled eight men when I walked in. They looked terrified. All were at least twenty-five years my senior. To them I was a well-known troublemaker, journalist and feminist activist. I felt decidedly unwelcome, I could not relate to anything that was discussed and decided I was not ready for party politics and that Fine Gael was certainly not ready for me.

Perhaps this is not too surprising because, as an activist feminist and freelance writer at the time, I would not have been an easy fit with the Fine Gael Taoiseach, Liam Cosgrave. I was often critical of Fine Gael policies on women's rights, family law and family planning. While my parents probably influenced my initial choice of party, as they supported Fine Gael, my later decision to join the party was motivated by Garret FitzGerald – his liberalism, his enthusiasm for change and the promise of a better Ireland.

My father, who retired from An Garda Síochána in 1956 and lived in Blackrock, was during the 1970s an ardent foot soldier for Fine Gael in the Dún Laoghaire constituency, his heroes being Taoiseach Liam Cosgrave, leader of Fine Gael and Liam Cosgrave's father, William T. Cosgrave, who had been Taoiseach in the 1920s.

Needless to say my dad and I were poles apart on virtually everything political and had heated arguments, in which neither of us convinced the other. But in my first campaign as a Fine Gael candidate, in the 1979 European Election, my father put all our differences behind him, campaigned enthusiastically and was obviously very proud, although I was unsuccessful on that occasion. Unfortunately, he died in December 1979, before my first electoral success in Dublin South in 1981.

One of the lessons Fine Gael learned from the 1977 general election campaign was the need for professionalism and creativity in future campaigns. This lesson was learned mainly from Fianna Fáil, whose campaign for that election was brisk, well organised, media-focused and colourful. Nothing like it had been seen outside an American presidential election. The 1977 coalition parties, on the other hand, had presented an image of tired grey men, over-dependent on voter loyalty and on their performance for the previous four-and-a-half years.

Garret FitzGerald recognised the importance of professional planning and knew the role high-powered media relations and advertising would play in future elections. His recruitment of Peter Prendergast as national organiser and Ted Nealon as public relations officer were inspired choices. In his autobiography *All in a Life* Garret wrote:

> At no point in the past had our party organisation ever matched the professionalism of Fianna Fáil and in opposition in the 1930s and 1940s it had declined rather than developed.
>
> Peter Prendergast's ambition was, by hook or by crook, to remedy this defect. Under his skilful but subtle, some would say Machiavellian guidance, Fine Gael was to reach and surpass in sheer professionalism its hitherto dominant rival. Such an achievement was not attained without trauma.

Peter Prendergast had a marketing background and set about selling Fine Gael product to the public. A total pragmatist, he set his targets early on and worked fiendishly hard to achieve them. He seemed to work night and day in every part of the country and never looked anything but weary and drawn. In my experience, he believed in consultation with politicians and candidates. But party activists soon realised that if this didn't achieve his objective, there were other routes he would take to achieve the desired result. He could slip a knife through constituency ribs and then go home for tea. Peter knew the party and the personalities well. But his focus was on the bigger picture of the next general election and he never let his eyes stray.

Peter had been an unsuccessful Fine Gael candidate in the 1973 general election. He knew that if the party were to make the critical breakthrough needed to get back into government, the constituency 'hatchers' would have to be dealt with,. These were the many Fine Gael TDs with a seat in four- and five-seat constituencies who dominated their local organisations and discouraged the emergence of other strong and electable candidates.

Other past trends were also scrutinised: selecting a candidate for contrived reasons, like their being a long-time Fine Gael supporter, or solely because they were a Protestant or working class. Electability became the single relevant criterion in those years. The strategy was to beef up every ticket. The 1979 European and local elections were only two years away; these were reality politics, not rehearsals. Though Peter was effective and his strategies brought the desired electoral results, he made few friends among the rank and file of the party due to the nature of his job and perhaps also his methods.

Changes in which Garret FitzGerald was instrumental

included acquiring an impressive new party headquarters in Upper Mount Street, Dublin, amendments to the Fine Gael constitution to extend decision-making to party membership and the establishment of Young Fine Gael. Although the Fine Gael women's group had not yet been formally established, women formed a majority of members in urban constituencies. Garret FitzGerald's support and encouragement for political women helped to maintain a positive public focus, which was reflected in the active and vocal women's movements of the time.

My route into Fine Gael constituency politics in 1978 was rather unorthodox. After Garret FitzGerald's election as leader of Fine Gael in 1977, his newly-appointed national adviser, Peter Prendergast, began headhunting potential candidates for the 1981 general election. My husband Brian was at that time an insurance broker and had regular business meetings with Peter Prendergast in Fine Gael headquarters in Mount Street headquarters. During visits my name would come up and my intentions vis-à-vis party politics discussed and second-guessed. Brian would duly relay all this back to me but I paid little heed. I had no enthusiasm for party politics, which I felt was slow and complex and not woman-friendly. My views were also relayed back to Peter Prendergast. But the 'courtship' continued and I eventually agreed to a meeting in Fine Gael headquarters. Peter put his cards on the table. He said he believed I could win a Dáil seat in a Dublin constituency and I agreed to have a go.

Shortly afterwards I became a member of the Billy Fox Branch of Fine Gael in Mount Merrion. Billy Fox was a young Fine Gael senator, a Presbyterian, who had been shot by the Provisional IRA in March 1974. Deirdre McDevitt, a friend from schooldays and a co-founder of AIM Group in 1971, was secretary of the branch and she did the essential hand-holding I needed to make sense of it all. Joining a party is not quite like joining anything else, at least not in my experience.

Having been proposed, seconded and ratified as a member, I set about understanding the political speak which party veterans used and the various networks and hierarchies of the party. While the members of our branch were a delightful bunch of people, friendly and good humoured, and I enjoyed working with them, I was certainly not flavour of the month with others in the Dublin South Constituency. Memories are long in politics at local level and grudges can be held fast. Many of the members who campaigned in the 1977 general election for their then bright hope Sean Barrett and saw him lose crucial votes to me as an independent candidate were none too trusting. Nor did they disguise their feelings.

I knew I would have to earn my spurs in the constituency to gain support. I took officer positions at branch and constituency levels, rolled up my sleeves and got involved in policy-making, research, fundraising and door-to-door canvassing. Soon I realised that my range of interests would have to be broadened. Whatever my personal political motivation might be – and it was emphatically women's rights – mainstream political involvement could not be based on a single issue. Indeed well-meaning acquaintances then and later told me that women's rights were a proper turn off and would hinder my building an essential support base. Dealing with local issues like pupil-teacher ratio, rubbish collection and getting phones into acres of new houses were the stuff of Dublin local politics in the late 1970s.

The deteriorating situation in Northern Ireland was a subject which was debated with considerable passion at many meetings. People felt a sense of hopelessness at Taoiseach Charles Haughey's lack of progress and his deteriorating relationship with then Prime Minister Margaret Thatcher. For the British Prime Minister, swamped in local battles, Northern Ireland seemed little more than a distraction.

Mainly our debates at meetings were about high unemployment, then running at 18 per cent of the workforce, and the emigration of young people. The sole Fine Gael Oireachtas representative in what was then the three-seater Dublin South County constituency was the late John Kelly, former Minister for Industry, who was Attorney General and Chief Whip in the 1973-7 coalition government. He was the front-bench spokesman on Industry and Commerce during my first years in the party and therefore the branch's conduit to the leadership.

Although John and I held vastly differing views on many social issues, not least contraception and divorce, and at times we seemed to have only local issues in common, on a personal level I found him good company, straight and fair as a constituency colleague. I know John found it difficult and uncomfortable to adapt to the leadership change from Liam Cosgrave to Garret FitzGerald. He was very much in the traditional Fine Gael mould. He did not trust the Labour Party and disliked its quasi-socialism. He argued strenuously against creating a 'nanny' state and on many occasions chided Fine Gael for being over-enthusiastic liberals, thereby handing the conservative vote to Fianna Fáil. But he need not have worried: as I was to discover, Fine Gael conservatives were alive and well and not all living in rural Ireland. John also felt that Fianna Fáil and Fine Gael should put Civil War politics behind them. There were few if any supporters for his proposal that the two major parties should form a grand coalition, having sought out the common ground that obviously existed between them, and govern Ireland into prosperity and peace. The matter was never debated, nor did either party give John any encouragement, but this did not stop him airing his proposal at regular intervals.

John Kelly was a celebrity constituency colleague; competent and colourful on television and radio discussions. He was one of the few Dáil speakers for whose speeches colleagues stayed in the chamber. Although his background was one of privilege, he related to all levels of Fine Gael (and many Fianna Fáil) voters. Just how popular he was I discovered when visiting party councillors in every constituency in the 1987 Seanad election campaign. John Kelly's complimentary letter of introduction, which had gone ahead of me to all councillors, helped me win a seat on the Labour panel, in what was a difficult election. From Kerry to Donegal I heard yarns about John and realised that despite his South County Dublin image, his personality and humour crossed all frontiers.

It was make-up-your-mind time for me when I was asked early in 1979 to put my name forward for the Dublin constituency selection for the first directly elected

European Parliament. But as was so often the case the joy of the opportunity was overshadowed by anxiety and guilt about the family. Winning a seat would mean long absences from home and how would the children, then aged ten, fourteen and seventeen, cope?

Of the three children, Amanda, at ten, would have been most directly affected: working as I did from a home office, I was always on hand for her. More immediately I was concerned about Jacqueline, who at seventeen was due to begin her Leaving Cert on 7 June, polling day. Back in the 1970s, Irish society did not have the broad-based acceptance of a mother's role outside the home that exists now. However in our family we always approached serious issues through round-table discussion and my candidacy was thus decided. If I ran, it would be with the serious objective of winning a seat, in which event I would be in Brussels or Strasbourg all week, every week.

It was not a rosy prospect for children used to a traditional close-knit family. While Jacqueline's focus was her Leaving Certificate at that point, she was totally in favour. Garrett, now in his transition year, was over the moon at the thought of another campaign, and little Amanda, who understood least of all, was carried away by his excitement. As ever it was Brian's overwhelming support and encouragement that convinced me. He said that the combined efforts of family, friends, neighbours and party would make the campaign feasible and a seat in the European Parliament likely. So Jacqueline decamped to my parents' house for three months before her exam where she got care, quietness to study and her meals on time.

A team of family and friends organised a six-month family framework to free me for the campaign. I needed a crash course in European politics, procedures and law and began familiarisation trips to Brussels and Strasbourg, mainly to participate in events organised by the European People's Party, the group to which Fine Gael belonged. These briefings gave me a flavour of political work at European level but they were mostly talking shops, which I found dull and boring.

Nobody in the party mentioned money but I knew that a campaign of six months' duration would be costly, so I set about fundraising. Party colleague Monica Barnes of Dún Laoghaire had been selected as a candidate for Leinster and we contacted the European People's Party women's sector. They helped in practical ways, with campaign funds, literature and specific seminars that provided the women's focus on the Parliament. Canvassing for the EEC, as the EU was then known, was pushing an open door as far as most Irish women were concerned. Since Ireland's entry to the market in 1973 the role of women at work had systematically improved: European directives and other instruments on equal treatment and equal pay were the big sticks that forced successive Irish governments to prioritise women's rights.

By early 1979, with the blessings of those who mattered, I was on my way! A packed Fine Gael selection convention in the Mansion House in early 1979 ratified me as a candidate for Dublin, along with Richie Ryan and Maurice Manning.

My proposer was the late Jim Mitchell, who did the honours with his usual robust generosity, praising me to the heavens although I had never met him before that night. I had been cautioned not to mention women so my speech evoked the values and standards of the Fine Gael Party of my father, who was in the audience, and my belief that closer economic and political integration with Europe would not represent a threat to our identity or our values. The publicity next day was very positive.

With an electorate of 700,000 in Dublin city and county, we had very little door to-door canvassing. Instead there was lots of noise, music, colour, badges, hats and colour posters. We spent our days on the Fine Gael bus, travelling to meeting venues, shopping centres, schools, coffee mornings and after-Mass meetings. Garret FitzGerald and other senior party figures joined us whenever possible and Garret's wife Joan was a hugely entertaining fellow-traveller. When Garret was not around she tucked into the Ritchies mints which Richie Ryan kept on board for children.

The campaign was as unlike my DIY 1977 campaign as could be. The Fine Gael organisers were new to the razzmatazz of US-type electioneering. They felt there was much to gain and no holds were barred. Needless to say, it was all done at huge financial cost. The campaign was extremely professionally organised, there was constant back-up and support and nothing was left to chance. For me it was a case of learning on the run. I was very much the political novice and fortunate to have two fair and decent fellow-candidates, former Minister for Finance Richie Ryan and university lecturer, former senator and writer Maurice Manning.

Although the three of us focused at all times on

the EEC and the role of the European Parliament, on every possible occasion discussion reverted to local and national politics. People were angry with Fianna Fáil, because of a prolonged postal strike and a refuse strike, which occurred during the election campaign itself. Not surprisingly, bread-and-butter issues mattered more to the ordinary Irish voters than a distant parliament in Strasbourg. I recall the puzzlement of a Danish journalist accompanying a Garret FitzGerald group on a door-to-door walkabout in a new but poor Finglas estate, strewn with garbage. Why was the leader of a Christian Democrat Party seeking votes in a working-class area? He had yet to learn about the diversity of the Irish electorate and the complexities of proportional representation.

Voting for local councillors was held the same day as the European elections and double the number of women candidates as stood in the 1974 local elections were standing, both as independents and on party tickets. The WPA had again organised its campaign with lapel and car stickers, this time saying, 'More Power To Your Women'.

1979 was the year women took a huge political leap, spurred on and supported mainly by the energies and activities of the WPA and to a lesser extent by party leaders who saw possible benefits to harnessing the women's vote. On this occasion the WPA campaign was countrywide, embracing all women candidates, both party-affiliated and independent. The association built on its experience of the 1977 campaign and this brought substantial results, changing long-held attitudes, such as women voting for the same candidates as their husbands.

When I arrived at the count centre in Ballsbridge at midday on 10 June, Garret FitzGerald was there in a state of high anticipation. Elsewhere in the hall my father stood guard over an enormous bundle of my first preference votes, which he monitored through several counts over two days when it seemed that I might take a second seat for Fine Gael after the election of Richie Ryan. It was not to be: against the odds the Labour Party took two seats, with one each for Fianna Fáil and Fine Gael.

Garret was interviewed at the count for the *WPA Journal* and said: 'Anyone who tries to deny that there is a woman's vote after this is ignoring the reality and will certainly pay dearly for their mistake in the next election.' This gave me more than a little satisfaction.

The late Eileen Desmond of Labour and Sile de Valera of Fianna Fáil won two of the fifteen seats for the European Parliament. Monica Barnes and I performed remarkably well, coming within a whisper of winning seats. Fine Gael won four of the fifteen European seats and came out on top in the gender stakes in the local elections: 10 per cent of the party's local representatives were women.

Many of the women elected that day – Mary Flaherty, Alice Glenn, Nora Owen, Carrie Acheson, Madeleine Taylor-Quinn, Avril Doyle and Fianna Fáil's Mary O'Rourke – began apprenticeships as councillors which would bring them to the Dáil in the general elections of 1981-2. Senator Mary Robinson, then a member of the Labour Party, was elected to Dublin Corporation. For the first time women were elected in every local authority. For women, the results of the European and local elections of 1979 were causes for celebration and an indication of victories to come.

As the 1981 general election approached no effort was spared and no job was too difficult or too menial for Fine Gael party members. Never before had such large numbers, with women and young people in the majority, turned out, joined branches, attended meetings and contributed in practical ways. Fine Gael was flavour of the month. Many people were attracted by the idealism and vision of Garret FitzGerald. He brought a new excitement to ordinary politics with his vision for change.

People were tired of the opportunism of Fianna Fáil, their awarding of jobs and contracts to their supporters and their toadying to the Catholic Church on social issues. There was public unease at the state of the public finances, inflation was running at 20 per cent, unemployment was at an all-time high of 18 per cent and there was stalemate in the Northern Ireland Troubles. It was felt that reforms would come only through a change of government and Fine Gael was prepared to do whatever it took to win votes to that end.

My first wounds of political battle were inflicted, or indeed self-inflicted, on 11 March 1981, at the Dublin South selection convention for the general election. As most practising politicians know, the bloodiest battles are waged well before polling day – the battles to get on the party ticket.

According to the Fine Gael system of the time, delegates from each of the nineteen branches were mandated at their respective meetings to select four candidates. At the convention, each prospective candidate was proposed and seconded and then made speech. But in hindsight this was little more than window-dressing and a night out. The die had already been cast in the pubs and parlours of the delegates. The convention was only a formality.

As well as myself, the candidates included John Kelly TD, councillor and solicitor Alan Shatter, councillor Alexis Fitzgerald, councillor Tommy Hand, councillor Myles Tierney and Anne O'Connell, a Dáil secretary and constituency activist. When the convention votes were counted, lo and behold, four men – Kelly, Shatter, FitzGerald and Hand – had won. I was deeply disappointed, as I realised that there were facts about politics that the WPA couldn't teach, like the tendency of convention delegates to lie and the patronage network utilised by men. After the convention Brian and I had a drink with friends and went home deflated.

Later that night Catherine Meehan, Garret Fitz-Gerald's personal assistant, arrived at the house with a letter from Garret saying how disappointed he was with the result and that he hoped I would accept co-option.

Newspaper reporters who attended the convention had a field day next morning. Press and radio journalists pursued me looking for a quote. What hope, they asked, for women in politics, when the most liberal party in the most liberal constituency in the country chose four male candidates? The Dublin South constituency executive was none too pleased to be the focus of such unfavourable national publicity so near the general election but Garret had moved fast. I accepted his offer to co-opt me and the rest is history. In politics winning absolves all sins. I won the second of three Fine Gael seats in Dublin South in the general election of June 1981. The next stop was Dáil Éireann.

The weeks between the election on 11 June and the first sitting of the Dáil on 30 June were like a honeymoon. Our house was full of flowers, letters and cards. This reinforced my sense of achievement and importance. If I had moments of doubt or concern about starting a job I knew nothing about, these did not come until later. I quickly assumed the persona of a politician, enjoying the high public recognition and the media interest. On a practical level I set about employing a housekeeper and bought a mint-green dress and jacket for my first day of public office.

Every TD gets gallery tickets for the first formal sitting of a new Dáil, and for a first-time TD these are precious indeed. When my mother, who was one of my guests, started to cry just as she arrived, I told her it was no day for tears but an occasion for joy and optimism. But I know her tears were for my late father. Few other events in life are charged with such emotion and sense of achievement as winning a Dáil seat in a general election. If you share the moment with family, colleagues and friends it is all the richer. Brian and the children were bursting with pride for me and felt part of my success.

8

WELL DONE, HUGH!

It was my first working day in Leinster House and my first parliamentary party meeting after the general election success. The bright June sun streaming through the high windows of the party room matched the mood of the sixty-five new and returning deputies engaged in noisy introductions and reunions. The party chairman, Kieran Crotty, opened the meeting with a roll call and people stood as names were called. When new TD, Mary Flaherty, a pretty young blonde woman, stood up in the front row, someone said, 'Well done, Hugh,' the implication being that Hugh Byrne, her constituency colleague was responsible for 'bringing her in'. In fact, Doctor Hugh Byrne, who was commended by the wag from the west, had received fewer first preference votes than Mary.

Initially I felt that all of us first-time elected women were regarded as a sort of aberration, a new untested breed of uncertain origin, probably in only temporary tenancy in Leinster House. I clearly remember how uncomfortable and lonely I was during these first weeks in Dáil Éireann, a strange male club, which felt like a

124

political locker-room. Nothing in my experience up to then, either in my work life or within organisations, had prepared me for politics. It was difficult to find a level on which to communicate with male TDs, a difficulty I suspect they shared when trying to communicate with me. At that time, when you signed on as a newly elected TD in the Ceann Comhairle's office, you were given a copy of the Irish *Constitution* into one hand and the standing orders for Dáil Éireann into the other. After that you were on your own. The implication was that elected representatives must know everything. But you didn't!

Working conditions in the 22nd Dáil were challenging. For the first few months, I shared office space with five other new TDs. Our room had heretofore been a public room, used for meetings. Now each of us had just about space enough for a desk and a filing cabinet. The severe lack of women's toilets anywhere near the Dáil chamber told its own story: it was several years before any were installed. An interesting concession to women members was a small carpeted room, with a mirror and armchairs, on the ground floor. It could have been a genteel ladies' sitting room, although genteel we women TDs were certainly not – and we had little time to sit there. Even if we had chosen to have a meeting there, fourteen elected women would not have fitted in at the same time. Only one of the newly-elected rural TDs appeared to use it regularly. She made no secret of the fact that she was very unhappy in her new role and indeed served only one short term. When the room was reclaimed for general use, we did not miss it.

This is not to say that the remainder of the accommodation was adequate, particularly as, unlike nowadays, we were absolutely confined to Leinster House by party whips during sitting hours, from 10.30 am to 9.00 pm. During the daily debates, losing a vote on a substantive issue could lead to a snap general election and the Fine Gael-Labour coalition was working with a majority of one vote. Only during the daily hour of question time was it was fairly safe to leave the House.

While the members' bar was comfortable and relaxing, in those years women members did not frequent it. Being the only woman member present is fine until some man decides to share anti-woman jokes, which was my unhappy experience more than once. All this was before the days of political correctness and in truth the jokes often discomfited the other men present, even if they remained silent. This behaviour had what I believe was the desired effect on me: I stayed away! I ceased to regard the member's bar as a place in which to relax and it was some time before I ventured back.

The serious business for me was getting on with the work I wanted to do. Getting someone to brief me on how the system worked was my priority. Once I was settled in and well before the new Dáil term began in the autumn, I persuaded the clerk of the Dáil to organise familiarisation sessions for new TDs. From the large turnout on the day it seemed that others were as mystified as myself. Knowing only the theory of how parliament works is like having a car without an engine. It took at least a year before I mastered the Dáil machine: understanding how to use question time to best effect, how to get private members' debating time and generally comprehending the complexity of our parliamentary system. With three general elections in eighteen months I also developed considerable campaigning expertise.

On Tuesday 30 June I sat in the Dáil chamber for the first time and watched Garret FitzGerald being elected Taoiseach by eighty-one votes, the combined votes of Fine Gael and Labour TDs, as well as Jim Kemmy, a new independent TD. I decided that politics could never be better than this, as we watched the new cabinet appointments being announced. Three ministers were only thirty-four years old: the late Jim Mitchell, Minister for Justice, the late John Boland, Minister for Education, and John Bruton, Minister for Finance,. On his first day in the Dáil, Alan Dukes became Minister for Agriculture at the age of thirty-six.

But this blissful new dawn was to herald a period of stress and difficulty, which led into another general election. This would snatch everything away before the end of that year. Apart from the fact that the new Fine Gael-Labour Coalition government inherited from the previous Fianna Fáil administration a financial crisis, unprecedented levels of public borrowing and very high unemployment, the spectre of the H-Block hunger strike in Northern Ireland dominated political consciousness and public opinion in those early months of the new government.

As part of the campaign to secure political status for the IRA's paramilitary prisoners, which included the hunger strikers, H-Block candidates had stood in twelve constituencies in the 1981 general election. Two prisoners,

Paddy Agnew and Kevin Doherty, won Dáil seats. The hunger strike began on 1 March 1981 and ended on 3 October that year after eleven men had died.

The 22nd Dáil did not last much longer than the hunger strike. In the months between its first meeting in June 1981 and its dissolution in January 1982, there was an overall sense of tension, even desperation, about the state of the public finances. Tough measures were needed if the economic crisis was to be tackled and this meant unpopular cutbacks. Fine Gael and Labour members alone would not get us through essential but unpopular votes in the Dáil: the government was vulnerable and we all knew it. As the government worked with a bare majority and depended on the votes of independents there was a surreal atmosphere around Leinster House. Not at all a good way in which to establish a political career, given the paranoia politicians feel about elections. It was with some relief that we got to August and the long summer recess.

The Dáil returned from the summer break on 28 October and I made my maiden speech, anxious to put my political intentions on the record. I expressed the main concerns of Irish women, from health and maternity needs to retraining women to re-enter the workforce and the updating of family law. I spoke at some length about Fine Gael manifesto proposal to give a tax credit of £9.60 per week, – £500 per annum – to wives who worked solely in the home. Addressing my colleagues I said:

> Most deputies can never realise what this modest sum will mean to many women. Whether we

> like it or not, society's measure of one's worth
> has always been in terms of financial recognition
> for work done. This allowance establishes the
> principle that women have rights to financial
> reward the same as anyone else.

Wives and mothers had come out with prams and toddlers on a wet polling day in June to vote for this proposed allowance. For the first time a payment, however small, was to be vested directly in women at home. Because there was no data available on women who had no income of their own, they were invited to apply for the credit.

Fianna Fáil had discredited the measure during the election campaign, even to the extent of billboard advertisements telling male voters: 'Men, Fine Gael are making advances to your wife and they are doing it with your monies.' I felt it was a tawdry, shortsighted ploy for political gain. But it worked, by instilling doubts and fears in male voters. The majority of women did not apply for the scheme as a result of confusion about how it would work and in the subsequent government Fianna Fáil was conveniently able to drop the measure.

During the Dáil session of autumn 1981 we felt the first sharp edge of media. In a piece in *Status* magazine in October 1981 called 'Summer of Silence', Nell McCafferty aimed a swingeing blow at all the newly-elected women politicians. Nell was a good and experienced journalist and must have known the nature of a post-election Dáil, not to mention the fact that the Dáil and Seanad had spent four months on summer recess.

Because we were new girls on the block, women deputies attracted a great deal of media attention in the early years but most of it was informed, fair comment, rooted in an understanding of how parliamentary politics works. I had cause to regret the often wildly inaccurate material produced by columnists who made no contact with me to establish facts and were ignorant about how politics operates and policies are implemented, but expected instant results in every area from childcare to contraception.

The routine for an ordinary backbencher (as opposed to the front-bench team) was pretty uninspiring. As long as you appeared for votes and always followed the party line you were left alone. Backbenchers see very little of the action, no matter what political events on a global or national level are happening or being planned. Our main forum for communication was the weekly parliamentary party meeting, which could be tense and argumentative, particularly when our party was in government. Many colleagues used the meetings to cut ministers and even the Taoiseach down to size. For P.J. Sheehan of Cork or the late delightful Willie O'Brien of Limerick, politics were about farm subsidies, a hospital bed or an old-age pensioner and no matter that the minister at the top table had issues of national or even international concern on his mind, or had just come back from an all-night meeting in Brussels. Despite tenacious questioning by some TDs, backbenchers learned little of ongoing government plans, mainly due to a culture of secrecy around government matters at that time but also to prevent controversial issues being leaked to the media after the meetings.

There was guaranteed to be a battle if the local press announced some innovation (school, hospital, road by-pass) in a deputy's constituency or, horror of horrors, by a Fianna Fáil colleague, before a government backbencher could take the credit locally by being the first to know. The importance of TDs' getting individual credit for local developments was something that baffled me at first but I grew to understand that under our system it is a powerful currency. We were elected to make thing happen, to fulfil expectations and to get results: that to me was the bottom line.

The coalition government's first budget in January 1982 was, with hindsight, doomed, depending as it did for crucial votes on the support of independent deputies. There was a presumption among party strategists that independent TDs like Jim Kemmy and Sean Dublin Bay Loftus would vote with us, rather than face losing their seats in a snap general election. In the end both deputies voted with Fianna Fáil, Jim Kemmy because he could not support the extension of VAT to clothing and shoes.

It was a gamble and we lost. On a crucial financial vote we lost by eighty-one votes to eighty-two. Losing a Dáil vote on a financial resolution or other substantive issue inevitably means a general election, unless the government can win a subsequent motion of confidence.

In *All in a Life*, Garret FitzGerald claims he felt 'happy and exhilarated by the events of that night' but no one I knew shared that feeling. My recollection of that dramatic evening is of sheer frustration that we had not managed things better. One colleague remembers me sitting crying on the lobby steps after the vote was announced and the implications of the forthcoming general election hit home. I was probably dreading facing another bruising selection convention in Dublin South.

When Garret came to the party room after the Dáil defeat he faced a demoralised parliamentary party, although he and John Bruton were in upbeat, bullish form. They set out an analysis of what had happened and why it was impossible to compromise on the public finances. Surprisingly, there were few recriminations. Despite their collective anxieties most TDs had confidence that Garret's leadership and his public appeal would be able to defend our position on the economy.

All the parliamentary party meetings in that short Dáil of 1981-2 had been dominated by national economic issues. In his regular homilies to us John Bruton said we could not go on sugaring the pill of public finances – we were fooling people and fooling ourselves. The country's situation was indeed critical: our ability to borrow abroad was at risk and in 1981 two-thirds of total income tax revenue was spent on servicing our foreign debt. John Bruton, who was at his best in those years as Minister for Finance, must have been glad to have the chalice of the economy pass from him. The question was whether we could increase the number of Fine Gael seats countrywide in the impending elections, to enable us to survive without the support of independent TDs and take necessary if unpopular economic decisions.

Our instruction on that day in January 1982 was to get ourselves re-elected, to canvass vigorously on our budget and to show the electorate how Fine Gael would tackle the financial crisis – simple as that.

As we left for our constituencies Monica Barnes noted aloud that at least bread, flour and margarine subsidies had not been touched. I thought that had precious little relevance for voters in either of our better-heeled constituencies, her Dún Laoghaire or my Dublin South.

How different the lead-up to this general election of 1982 was from that of the previous year. There was no nail-biting selection conventions because the three-hundred-strong constituency convention called at two days' notice approved the candidacy of sitting deputies, John Kelly, Alan Shatter and myself by acclamation. My team of women canvassers braved the cold, grim January weather to cover the constituency during the day and our branch, now chaired by Kevin Norton, was better organised than ever.

We campaigned on our defeated budget and, unbelievably, constituents were remarkably tolerant and understanding. Pre-election leadership polls showed that Garret FitzGerald was way ahead of Charles Haughey. This lead held up during the campaign and was a great comfort for Fine Gael candidates. Sile de Valera, who had unsuccessfully contested the 1981 general election in Dublin South, was on the Fianna Fáil ticket again. Her main platform was Northern Ireland and while her republican views kept her in the media glare, they did not go down well with Dublin South voters. I know she was very badly treated on the constituency's doorsteps.

In truth, while no politician welcomes a snap election, we were all rather relieved to see the end of that grim twenty-second Dáil. Although life as a TD was tough and demanding, I found that I was well and truly hooked.

All that goes with being an elected party representative challenged my sense of independence as by nature I was not a team player: I liked to take solo runs on issues about which I felt strongly. I discovered that perceptions of me appeared somehow to have changed during my eight months as a politician. I noted in my journal how fascinated men were and that when I was out socially they talked endlessly to me about politics. On the other hand, their wives, or many of them, treated me like a dalek. They remained quiet and distant, unable to relate to the political world I now occupied. I made a resolution that if I got re-elected my objective would be to demystify politics for women and make them realise just how deeply politics influenced their lives and the lives of their families.

If a first electoral success is sweet, the second is sweeter still. In February 1982, Dublin South Constituency again returned John Kelly, Alan Shatter and myself on the Fine Gael ticket. We lost two seats nationwide, down from sixty-five to sixty-three, while Fianna Fáil gained three, up from seventy-eight to eighty-one, while Labour remained at fifteen. This amounted to a hung Dáil, so the major parties began intense negotiations with four independents and three Sinn Féin Workers' Party. Unfortunately, my party colleagues Madeleine Taylor-Quinn and Alice Glenn lost their seats but were to be re-elected in the second general election of 1982. Gemma Hussey, a very ambitious and determined woman, then an NUI Senator, was elected to the Dáil for the rural constituency of Wickow, although she lived in Dublin 6.

9

THE GUBU DÁIL

Back we came to Leinster House after the February 1982 general election. Fine Gael had been beaten but only just. It was a good feeling for me to have been returned by Dublin South, although this time we had none of the fun and festivities of the previous June. When I went into Leinster House to find an office, the bars and corridors were rife with rumour and gossip. Everyone wanted to give you their predictions for the next administration and get yours. I felt that politics was going to be very different from what it had been up to this.

Well before the new Dáil met, a deal would have to be hammered out between the parties, as neither Fianna Fáil nor Fine Gael had an overall majority. There was nothing really strange about this: most European countries had had coalition governments for many years. But it was new for Fianna Fáil. The arithmetic rather favoured Mr Haughey. Fianna Fáil had eighty-one seats, so he needed three or four more votes to ensure his election as Taoiseach to the 166-member Dáil. He set out on a charm offensive to woo those votes, entering negotiations with three Sinn Féin The Workers' Party deputies and newly-elected independent TD Tony Gregory. On the other hand Garret FitzGerald only half-heartedly undertook negotiations to gather support. He knew too well that keeping the support of independents would involve considerable public spending. Having recently presided over the nation's soaring national debt, Garret knew first hand the precarious state of our finances. How could he have justified 'buying' power back? Some Fine Gael colleagues felt that he should do just that and several pointed out the risks of letting Charles Haughey and the Fianna Fáil party back in government at the levers of the economy. Mr Haughey had no such reservations and we watched his deal unfold in the Dáil chamber on the first day of the 23rd Dáil.

It was Tony Gregory, the brand-new independent deputy from Dublin Central, who scored the bull's-eye. In a lengthy speech he listed the goodies he had been promised, among them housing, a community school for the inner city and a National Development Agency, at a total cost of at least £150 million. In return for this bounty he walked through the lobby to elect Charles Haughey Taoiseach and continued to vote with Fianna Fáil. Tony Gregory's grateful constituency returned him to Dáil Éireann at every general election since then until his death in 2009. As well as Gregory and the Workers' Party, Haughey received the support of the Donegal independent TD Neil Blaney. Not what anyone could call stable government.

Once more I realised that my working life was to be dominated by three-line whips. Each week the notice of business for the coming week in the Dáil – known as the 'whip' – was sent to our homes by the party chief whip. Thick black underlining (three times – hence 'three-line whip') warned of votes at any time (except question time), for which we *must* be in the Dáil chamber. This meant staying around Leinster House, at least within earshot of the division bells. Missing a vote was a mortal sin in politics and could have devastating consequences, if the lost vote was on a financial motion or a vote of principle. Even ministers on state business were not excluded and had to seek a 'pair' along with the rest of us. (This meant that two deputies on opposite sides of the house could miss votes by agreement with the whips.) Pairs were not granted easily in those days, due to lack of trust and cooperation between government and opposition parties.

Lack of goodwill between party whips often resulted in their being precious little leeway on votes. This caused a problem for me during 1982. I had been advised by my obstetrician in January of that year that I needed a hysterectomy and I decided not to put it off for much longer. Healthwise, I was way under par, after a hard-fought election. I was exhausted and very anaemic. So in early May 1982 I went into Mount Carmel, a small private hospital in South Dublin run by a nursing order, and had my operation and three glorious weeks' rest.

But politics of a different type were not far away. A young mother from the next ward, who had also been admitted for a hysterectomy, asked to see me. She had been on the operating table, already anaesthetised, with the surgical team about to start the operation, when a senior sister checked her chart, saw that she was married and only thirty-six and refused to cooperate any further as a matter of principle. Back she was wheeled to her ward, uterus intact, very angry that a nurse's moral preference took precedence over her health and medical needs.

While I was on sick leave I was appointed to the Fine Gael front bench as spokesperson on women's affairs. This involved attending front-bench meetings, speaking in the Dáil on legislation related to women and preparing party policies. I saw it as wonderful new challenge and resolved to become more familiar with the parliamentary system and to establish easier relationships with party colleagues. I felt, however, that I would never win over some of these, partly because of my reputation as a feminist activist but also because they had never regarded women's affairs as a serious issue.

Recording my time on the front bench, I wrote in my journal:

> I am very unlikely to be part of a future Garret government. Front-bench meetings are badly run. Garret rambles all over the place and can be very distracting in serious discussions. Alan Dukes is the most ambitious (also most capable) man around the table. He has a razor-sharp brain and great decisiveness and sometimes uses ridicule to defeat opposition arguments. He is tough. John Bruton is much the same but softer. He concedes more easily, listens to counter-arguments and compromises. An indefatigable worker and totally dedicated to politics.

There was nothing before or since that I can compare to that short-lived twenty-third Dáil. In every way it was Mr Haughey's show. Almost immediately a new aura of control was obvious, whereby any criticism or opposition to him was portrayed as a conspiracy, almost anti-national. The simmering resentment of TDs like Charlie McCreevy, Mary Harney and Jim Gibbons found an outlet in the media and inevitably lead to challenges to Mr Haughey's leadership. Whenever heckling broke out in the chamber, which it did regularly, usually on the order of business, Mr Haughey would silence the Fianna Fáil benches in seconds with one Mussolini-like gesture.

Charles Haughey was a small, serious man, who walked with a magisterial gait. As I watched him across the Dáil I wondered if the rumours about him were true. Did he really have a mistress? Was he, as alleged, indebted to Allied Irish Bank to the tune of a million pounds? Thanks to the McCracken and Moriarty tribunals we now know the extent of Mr Haughey's double standards and his extraordinary approach to ethics in public office. There was a climate of fear and intimidation in the party under his leadership, confirmed by some Fianna Fáil colleagues over late-night drinks in the bar.

Within months of the general election events were to become even more extraordinary. When, during the summer of 1982, a suspected murderer was discovered hiding in the attorney general's apartment in Dún Laoghaire, Mr Haughey, briefing journalists, called the situation 'grotesque, unbelievable, bizarre and unprecedented', and former minister and journalist Conor Cruise O'Brien coined the term 'GUBU'. I felt it described exactly the odd events and the strange behaviour of Fianna Fáil supporters throughout those months. On many occasions the Dáil public rooms seemed like a fairground, with heaving bodies, many the worse for wear and very rowdy as the rank and file attempted to sort out the problems inside the party. This was particularly noticeable before and during the heaves against Mr Haughey, with encounters sometimes ending with fisticuffs. I never hung around after late debates as the atmosphere was so charged and nasty.

Although a veteran of two general elections, I still regarded myself as a novice TD. Being on the opposition benches is a very different type of political life from belonging to the government party. Again it was a learning process. Some interesting scores were settled during our own parliamentary party meetings. According to party rules the leadership is subject to a secret ballot after each general election. Few had doubts about Garret's position but there were six dissenters. One of these was Austin Deasy, who made a very emotive speech. He accused Garret of dropping him from the cabinet once Fine Gael got into government in 1981 and of not speaking to him for eight months. I found it all quite a revelation but it ended well for Austin: he was given the Foreign Affairs brief in the shadow cabinet and in the next administration performed very creditably as Minister for Agriculture.

Equally bitter was the row caused by Dick Burke's acceptance of the position of European Commissioner from Charles Haughey. This created a vacancy in Dublin West, causing a by-election and the prospect of the loss of a Fine Gael seat – not a happy prospect for any of the members of the new parliamentary party. The background was that Fianna Fáil's Michael O'Kennedy, who had been commissioner since 1981, resigned to contest and win a seat in the general election of January 1982. Charles Haughey's ploy was to send Dick Burke to Europe, call a by-election for Dublin West, win the seat for Fianna Fáil and reduce or end his dependence on the Workers' Party.

When the news was relayed to our parliamentary party meeting, bedlam ensued. Dick Burke bowed in the face of the tidal wave of hostility and outrage, which, amazingly, seemed to surprise him. Most regarded his decision as incomprehensible – Jim Mitchell more than anyone. He had accepted Dick Burke on the ticket in his own constituency and worked hard to get him elected. Dick Burke, stung by the reaction of his colleagues, agreed to turn down the post. However, within days he had changed his mind again and accepted the job.

The parliamentary party issued a statement about the situation, which was not tough enough for Jim Mitchell, and then moved on. The redoubtable Jim straight away set about sourcing a by-election candidate. Enter Liam Skelly, a complete unknown, who ran against Fianna Fáil's Eileen Lemass and won the seat in May 1982. This was a poke in the eye for Charles Haughey and a major morale boost for Fine Gael.

By the time the Dáil returned after the summer recess, it was clear to all that this self-interested, manipulative government should not continue. Another challenge to Charles Haughey's leadership was due on 1 October and once again the atmosphere in Leinster House was heavy with intimidation and threats. Grassroots Fianna Fáil members roamed the corridors and bar campaigning for support for Charles Haughey. It was difficult not to get caught up in the gossip and intrigue and I wondered if I was the only one deeply concerned for the neglected affairs of state and the dire condition of our economy. Once more Charles Haughey won the leadership challenge, with fifty supporters and twenty-two opposed.

By now it was a deck chairs on the *Titanic* situation. The government party was bitterly divided and the main opposition parties were circling for the kill. With good reason. Rumours flew about regarding the behaviour of the Minister for Justice and his abuse of office for personal advantage. Worse still, anecdotal information was circulating about the illegal tapping of the phones of two political journalists. The end came with little drama when Fianna Fáil lost a Dáil vote by eighty votes to eighty-two. They were vulnerable on the day as one deputy, Doctor Bill Loughnane, had recently died and another, Jim Gibbons, was seriously ill and could not attend for the vote. So Charles Haughey's carefully stacked pack of cards came tumbling down. Politics is indeed about timing and luck.

I reflected on what a strange job I had. Normally a general election is held every four to five years, yet here I was in October 1982 heading into my third election campaign within eighteen months. The confidence I felt on this occasion was not misplaced: Fine Gael and Garret FitzGerald were at their highest poll rating, our election manifesto was practical and realistic and I greatly enjoyed the campaign. Once more, John Kelly, Alan Shatter and I won seats for Fine Gael in Dublin South. In the country as a whole Fine Gael came back with seventy seats and 39 per cent of the overall vote. Dick Spring, the new leader of the Labour Party, and his colleagues agreed a programme for government with Fine Gael and on 14 December 1982 Garret FitzGerald was once more elected Taoiseach, with eighty-five votes to seventy-nine.

10

Ms Minister and All That

As is the norm, the new cabinet was announced by newly appointed Taoiseach Garret FitzGerald. All the Fine Gael heavy hitters were there: Paddy Cooney, John Bruton, Peter Barry, Alan Dukes, John Boland, Jim Mitchell and Michael Noonan, with the addition of Gemma Hussey as Minister for Education and Austin Deasy as Minister for Agriculture.

I was feeling heroic because I had won a seat in another general election and pleased that the coalition being in power meant that we could hope for a proper Dáil that would last five years. But the future would be very tough, given the dire state of Ireland's economy and if I had any doubts about that, I had only to refer to the notes of one of John Bruton's parliamentary party speeches of the previous months:

> If we do not take action, it will be imposed on us. Our objective has to be to spread the sacrifices as evenly as possible, change existing taxes, plan new forms of taxation. We have gained our credibility as a party with a pledge

to set the national finances in order. We cannot
go on indefinitely sugaring the pill, fooling
people, least of all ourselves.

But Christmas 1982 was coming, Fine Gael was in
power and presumably we had the answers, so I danced
and partied with the rest. When Garret sent for me and
asked me to become Minister of State for Women's Affairs
in his department I gulped and said yes. A little later he
also appointed me to the Department of Justice, with the
brief of family law reform. So there I was two days before
Christmas Eve, elevated beyond my wildest expectations
and not a little bewildered by the implications of it all.
Fresh from the Dáil chamber, as I was taking the short-
cut to the Taoiseach's Department, I was rushed off
my feet by a bevy of Garda drivers waiting to catch a
new junior minister. (At that time all ministerial drivers
were members of An Garda Síochána.) I resisted their
offers. I told them I would be driving myself, in my new
standard-range Citroën and otherwise using taxis. Sean
Barrett, Minister of State in the Taoiseach's department
and also chief whip, escorted me to my new office on
the third floor of Government Buildings. Walking up the
sweeping staircase with its gleaming brass bannister, I
thought, good, I won't be polishing that every day!
      Sean introduced me to the Secretary of the Depart-
ment, Pádraig Ó hUiginn, who made me feel that he had
nothing more important to do that day than brief me and
meet my requests. My carpeted office was just enormous,
as was the mahogany desk with two phones. There was
an impressive but empty book cabinet, a conference table

and chairs, coffee table, arm chairs, a chaise longue and of course a drinks cabinet. Two smaller offices adjoined mine, for my private secretary and advisers.

As we drank tea from china cups Mr Ó hUiginn (later addressed as Pádraig) explained how the system worked and the likely fit for my office and myself in the department. There had never been a government sector or department for women's affairs before, so no blueprint or plan existed. We were in a greenfield situation.

I related well to Pádraig Ó hUiginn, an affable and elegant civil servant in the *Yes Minister* mould. That first afternoon I was anxious to explore my role in the Department of Justice, where I was minister of state, so Mr Ó hUiginn escorted me there. The Department of Justice was intensely secretive, which was not surprising at the time, given the conflict in Northern Ireland and the activities of the IRA. The department had central responsibility for prisons, law enforcement, counter-terrorism, the courts, An Garda Síochána and many areas related to these.

We were ushered into the inner sanctum of department general secretary Andy Ward, the man who presided over all this important work. He was renowned for his reclusive nature and was blamed by the media for the forensic secrecy with which his department functioned. Introductions over, the meeting came to a deafening halt. He had no spare offices, he told us. I feel sure Andy Ward had weighty matters on his mind that day and it soon became obvious he wanted me in his department like a stone in his shoe. 'It would be best, Minister,' he said, 'as you have offices in the Taoiseach's building, to work from there and we will send over all necessary documents.'

It took about a second before I replied:

> The way it is, Secretary, I will be involved in complex family legislation which I believe requires me to work closely with officials in this department. I feel this cannot be done at a distance, therefore I would ask you to locate a desk – a large broom cupboard with a light and a phone would do for a start – to enable me to work under the Justice roof.

Within a week I was back in the Department of Justice, occupying a large, carpeted ministerial office, briefly used by Dick Spring in the 1981 government when he served as Minister of State for Law Reform. Some broom cupboard! I interviewed and appointed the late Anne Boland as my private secretary and during my term in the Department of Justice she was a most loyal and dedicated colleague. I set out a schedule for working: Fridays in the Department of Justice to plan legislation and otherwise I would be on third floor of Government Buildings in the Department of An Taoiseach.

Here I was, occupying a high-profile role of which there were great public expectations and I just did not know how or where to start. No blueprint existed, nor was there work in progress. Right then I was a team of one. Of the five excellent civil servants appointed to the women's affairs section, only two had previously worked in the equality area.

Every January I received a maroon Institute of Public

Administration desk diary with my name embossed in gold, which was very grand. It was in such a diary, in 1983, that I wrote my 'shopping list' of legislative initiatives for the next four years. Because I felt it would be most easily accomplished, first on the list was the Domicile and Recognition of Foreign Divorces Bill (to end dependent domicile of women), then the Status of Children's Bill (to abolish illegitimacy). The preparation of a government report for the 1985 UN Women's Conference to be held in Nairobi, Kenya, was also my responsibility.

Closest to my heart was the establishment of a new family mediation scheme, because I had seen the need for it while working with AIM Group and with Irish Women's Aid. Then, of course, there were two controversial referenda to face, one on abortion, the second on divorce. I had no direct responsibility for them but I was closely involved in the debates and meetings. Both subjects were high-voltage and in the remit of An Taoiseach and the ministers for Justice and Health.

The Irish Constitution of 1937 included a prohibition on the introduction of legislation for divorce (Article 41). This meant that legislators' hands were tied and only the Irish people in a referendum could decide to remove or retain this prohibition. If the people voted to remove the ban, the Oireachtas would be free to introduce a divorce law. Public opinion was firmly in support of the status quo and although an increasing number of people needed divorce it was on the political back burner at that time.

What was very much on the front burner was the subject of abortion. Up to then the Constitution had been silent on the subject of abortion However, an articulate and determined group of people had formed a very effective lobby seeking a constitutional referendum to prohibit a law to legalise abortion ever being enacted by the legislature. They brought their message into every parish and, frankly, they were pushing an open door. As they saw it, their timing, the early 1980s, was perfect. The Fine Gael and Labour parties were in government, both suspected of having liberal agendas, and, compared to the more compliant Fianna Fáil, were not to be trusted. The pro-life lobby extracted pre-election promises from party leaders Garret FitzGerald and Charles Haughey to hold the constitutional referendum.

No matter that in February 1983 there was a war in Northern Ireland, we had appalling unemployment, an unacceptable level of emigration, high inflation and high income tax – the only show in town appeared to be abortion! Certainly many of the women journalists had it at the top of their agendas for delivery and I became one of their targets. What was I doing about it?

During most of the first year of the government that took office at the end of 1982, we lived through the most controversial, divisive and bitter episode in contemporary Irish politics. On a personal level I was not in favour of abortion, as after three wanted pregnancies and much reading and thinking I could not reconcile myself with the procedure. But I did not agree with a constitutional ban, nor with preventing women from getting clear information on abortion or from travelling to procure one. Having earlier flirted with one of the emerging pro-life groups, I found that I profoundly disagreed with their core message and the bitter passions it evoked.

The Labour leader, Dick Spring, refused to commit his party to a referendum and made it plain in the programme for government that he reserved the option of a free vote for his parliamentary party, if legislation came before the Oireachtas. An altogether sensible approach, one many of us in Fine Gael wished Garret had chosen. Whenever he could, Charles Haughey upped the ante. Just before polling day in November 1982 he published his wording for the referendum: 'The state acknowledges the right to life of the unborn and, with due regard to the equal right to the life of the mother, guarantees in its laws to respect and as far as practicable by its laws to defend and vindicate that right.' This clause later became Article 40.3.3 of the *Constitution of Ireland*.

The pro-life groups were almost salivating with satisfaction and demanded that the referendum on abortion be held by 31 March 1983. Charles Haughey did not benefit and lost the general election. Barry Desmond of Labour was appointed Minister for Health in the coalition government and told his cabinet colleagues that he would not handle the abortion brief. So with the Labour Party effectively washing its hands of the abortion amendment and Charles Haughey pursuing it with gusto in opposition, the chalice passed to Garret. It fell to Michael Noonan, the new Minister for Justice, to carry the amendment baton. Not only was Michael presiding over a crisis-prone Department of Justice with heavy responsibilities, he represented the confraternity city of Limerick, whose bishop was the very conservative and articulate Doctor Newman. Some time previously I had interviewed the bishop. We discussed the Irish feminist movement and its objectives. He had read the feminist books and knew all the movers and shakers of the time. Doctor Newman assured me with great concern that if we got our way and women achieved equality it would have the effect of turning men into savages. We were on a very dangerous course indeed, he said.

(But then I was never big in the bishop stakes. At a reception after a New Year peace ceremony in Mount Argus not long after my appointment, I was in a group with Bishop Kavanagh and Dermot Ryan (then Archbishop of Dublin) when a photographer, Ruth Rodgers, approached the group to take a picture, Archbishop Ryan very pointedly stepped away. Afterwards I asked him why he felt such a public snub was necessary and said that what he had done was unacceptable to me. He said, 'I do not share your views. I could not be photographed with you.' I replied. 'But I have never met you, nor spoken to you. How do not know my views?' I suggested a meeting to talk about our differences but nothing came of it!)

So here we were, a new government, with crucial economic problems facing the country and the spectre of an abortion referendum top of the agenda. For a while Fine Gael was like the rabbit transfixed by the headlights. But proceed we did: we went through the most horrible seven months imaginable.

There was a low poll – less than 50 per cent – and two-thirds of the people who voted assented to the change in the Constitution. My constituency in Dublin South voted no, as did Monica Barnes's in Dún Laoghaire. I know that even some of the conservatives were surprised by the level of intolerance the exercise uncovered. Irish society became polarised, a situation that lasted for some years.

When I look back on the months of the campaign and debates and remember listening to the pro-life TDs taking women's bodies apart in speeches sprinkled with vaginas, ovaries and uteri, to prove points or make an impression down in the home parish, I think how unpleasant it all was. There was a great lack of Christian charity, much bigotry and many closed minds. Most women colleagues left the chamber for the main debate. I was taking the front bench for Michael Noonan, so I heard most of the speeches.

It is easily seen that I was only a wet week in politics but my feelings about it were: let's take on the Church and Fianna Fáil, let's abandon plans for a referendum and get on with the real work. But that attitude took no account of the die-hard pro-life deputies in our party and even in Labour, who would certainly vote with Fianna Fáil. Then there was Garret's signed agreement with the pro-life lobby, which he felt he had to honour. These are the stresses of political leadership: nothing is straightforward; all is compromise.

When I was appointed minister for state by Garret FitzGerald, he suggested that I set up an inter-departmental working party on women's affairs, the main objective of which would be to review the existing situation of women in Ireland and bring forward proposals for reform. I thought this was a grand idea and that I would end up with a clear picture of difficult areas where legislation was required and that I would systematically deal with them. This was not quite what was agreed by the terms of reference under which we worked:

> To review the existing situation in relation to
> measures affecting women's affairs and family
> law reform, identifying areas still requiring
> action, considering the best administrative
> measures to promote positive opportunities and
> facilities to enable women to participate more
> fully in the life of the community and generally
> monitoring developments and keeping progress
> under review.

I felt pretty certain this was a cul-de-sac but by then it was too late to do anything about it. Civil servants learn about these working parties on their first day and are very fond of them.

The first meeting of the working party was in February 1983 and the committee worked solidly for two years, until February 1985. The eleven-chapter report called *Agenda for Practical Action* was well received and contained valuable statistics and facts hitherto unknown about Irish women's lives. The report also contained two reservations from members. The first was the representative of the Department of Finance and the Public Service, saying that spending any money on the proposals in the report could not be justified. At the time this was almost standard for the Department of Finance. Their representatives on working parties or committees would sit in a corner and said no to all spending.

The representative of the Department of Justice wrote: 'Implications of those findings would in many cases be likely to have consequences that would be quite far-reaching and perhaps unwelcome. I feel constrained to express the view that the examination of the matters concerned failed to take adequate account of those likely consequences. This is a personal view and does not purpose to represent any departmental view.' He also refused to sign the report.

In January 1984 the tragic death of fifteen-year-old Anne Lovett of Granard, County Longford, was one of the most difficult occurrences during my years as a minister of state. She died on a Tuesday afternoon in a Marian grotto with her new-born son, also dead, beside her. News of the tragedy did not emerge until the newspapers of the following Sunday, by which time the funeral of the mother and baby was over. When, on Sunday morning, newspapers reported the tragedy for the first time, journalists and photographers contacted me for comment. I was in An Grianán adult education college in Termonfeckin, County Louth, with Ballyfermot woman Anne McStay and thirty women from her area, conducting a weekend of community development. When I was interviewed I spoke with all the anger I felt. I called for an enquiry, called it a disaster.

But this was not the party way. Back in Dublin the Cabinet nominated Gemma Hussey, who was Minister for Education, to appear on RTÉ and answer compère Brian Farrell's questions. But by this time the town of Granard was up in arms, angry at the insinuations and uncomfortable under media focus, They had no answers to questions such as: Who knew Anne Lovett was pregnant? Why had no one helped her? What kind of community was Granard? There was serious criticism of the college of the Sisters of Mercy, Anne's school, and its staff. Gemma's broadcast left us with no greater clarity. In her published diaries, *At the Cutting Edge*, Gemma wrote that she felt I would be annoyed at her intervention Yes, I was thoroughly disappointed, as much by the fact that she had not contacted me as that she had not found a way to say it as it was. Gemma and I had travelled a long way for women's rights – why were we now stuck at this impasse? At the same time I appreciated that Gemma was in a tight corner and that she would have had her own sad feelings about Anne Lovett.

During the 1980s I was one of three ministers for women's affairs in the EU and during a week spent visiting other EU parliaments, I met French minister Yvette Roudy. She had a very large department, a budget to go with it and was a large and formidable woman. When I met the legendary Simone Weil, a Holocaust survivor, in Strasbourg the next day, she described Madame Roudy rather disparagingly as 'a classical feminist'.

At the invitation of the Swedish Minister for Equality, Anna-Greta Leijon, I spent a week in that country. It proved to be a most interesting and most practical visit. Even then Swedish women enjoyed enviable laws and regulations. Parliamentary representation was 30 per cent and six out of twenty ministers were women. Paid maternity leave lasted for eight months, with time off for both parents if their children were sick. I was mad with envy! It was not just that the advances for women in Sweden were remarkable in comparison to Ireland; it was that they were part of the culture of Swedish society, accepted as the norm.

For me it was back to my battle zone. We were now

at half-term in the 24th Dáil and my difficulties with the enigmatic Secretary of the Department of Justice, Andy Ward, had not eased. He found it very difficult to accept my role and provided absolutely no support in advancing legislation. Our attitudes and our goals were miles apart. I know he disliked women who were too pushy and persistent but to make any progress I had to be this way. We were not a good combination. I also feel that Michael Noonan might have given me more support but at that point he and Garret FitzGerald were licking their wounds after the failure of the 1984 summit on Northern Ireland and Margaret Thatcher's graceless dismissal of the three options of the New Ireland report.

1985 was not an altogether bad year. The framework for the Status of Children Bill had been agreed, as well as the Conciliation or Mediation Scheme, so I could forge ahead with them. At last the government passed the Health (Family Planning) (Amendment) Bill in Spring 1985, giving all adults a legal right to contraceptives. It was a good day. Alice Glenn, Tom O'Donnell and Oliver J. Flanagan of Fine Gael Party voted against the bill, as did two Labour deputies. We had secured one reform on the liberal agenda but there were many still to go.

It was inevitable that pressure would now build up for action on divorce, This came from liberals in Fine Gael, the youth sector and the women's group, and also very much from the media. I have no doubt also that certain rural deputies were telling the Taoiseach: 'Never mind that auld divorce, it won't win elections.' Because divorce was prohibited by our Constitution, a referendum had to be held to secure the agreement of the people before new laws could be introduced. However we did not have the luxury of time. Already the 1987 general election loomed.

During 1985 our lives changed dramatically on a personal level. In April of that year Brian's company J.J. Fennell (insurance brokers) went into voluntary liquidation with all the unfortunate consequences this entailed. It was a grim time. Brian had to let staff go and chair the creditors' meeting, always an ordeal. For me there was the publicity, but most of that was straightforward. We dealt with the changes and cut down spending and soon Brian was working again. My confidence took a big punch, as my job was uncertain and our children were at an expensive time as regards their education. Family, neighbours and friends supported us in many ways and the three children showed great maturity about everything, all of which helped to put things into perspective.

But another first was coming around very quickly: the UN conference in Nairobi in Kenya to mark the end of the decade for women It was to be a reporting and policy-shaping conference, attended by delegations from all the United Nation member countries. I knew little enough about the United Nations and nothing at all about how to lead an official Irish delegation to present our report. But I quickly learned. My department produced an honest report, citing recent reforms for Irish women and indicating legislative changes in hand.

Arriving at Nairobi was not unlike being dropped into the middle of a mardi gras parade. I had never been to Africa so it hit all my senses at once. Mainly I was struck by the colours. There were flags, bunting and exotic flowers everywhere, shades that were reflected in the women's dress. It was extremely hot. Our ambassador, Mary Tinney, welcomed us and explained that I would be staying at the embassy residence which was out of town while the rest of the party was accommodated in a city hotel.

Not being adverse to the kind of pampering that one reputedly gets as the house-guest of an embassy, I was quite contented with this arrangement. Until that night, when around midnight a cacophony of barking hounds sounded below my window. The ambassador had earlier filled me in on the hounds that were let loose in every garden after dark. All were killers. When I asked her about living alone, with just one gardener, she took me to her bedroom and showed me the steel frame, hefty lock and steel door that protected her. Then she told me anecdotes about neighbours who had been blown, hacked or burned at night. We amicably agreed that I would move back to the city, which in any case was more convenient to the conference centre.

The conference itself was held in a massive hall and the Irish table was in close proximity to those of Iran and Iraq. The women from these Islamic countries, to whom I would love to have spoken, were top to toe in black and did not fraternise at all. We worked through a paper produced by the UN. I can understand why such UN conferences seldom if ever reach agreement – they are so big and unwieldy and very diverse. I was certainly confused at first between resolutions in square brackets and round brackets, indicating what was agreed and what was not.

Over the years the UN has kept a watching brief on how member governments develop rights and policies for women and as such has been a real champion for women. Providing venues like Nairobi for representatives of the world's women to come together for both informal and official discussion was a huge resource, which individual countries could never have contemplated providing. We attended African women's markets, saw the development of their small industries, met local women MPs and really enriched our knowledge base. Seldom have I found such enthusiasm and generosity as I found among that vast crowd.

We accepted a long-standing invitation from the All China Women's Federation to visit China for their National Day, on 1 October 1985. Although twenty-five years have passed since our visit, we saw at that time strong signs of the prosperity China has since achieved. A three-hour journey on the Pearl River brought us to Canton, a vast, exciting if very humid city. In the Banphi restaurant the greeting ritual began with introductions and short speeches, then a twelve-course meal, during which spontaneous toasts to friendship and peace were drunk with local wine. It was a moment of truth for those who had forks and spoons in handbags. Chopsticks were just right for Chinese food and the cutlery stayed put.

During our stay we went to historical monuments and museums, to concerts and operas. I had asked in advance to see inside a prison and so we did, in Shanghai. The chief warden took us on a tour of the eighty-year-old British-built complex. A splendidly turned-out prisoner orchestra played the 'Blue Danube Waltz' and 'Stars and

Stripes Forever' in the main square. We were told that three hundred prison officers cared for 3,800 prisoners, all of whom worked a seven-day fifty-six-hour week in the garment factory. We watched as the T-shirts and track suits they produced were boxed and dispatched.

In the cities young people sidled up to us and tried to tell us about their lives in English. But no great exchanges were possible, as there was always a government 'minder' at our elbows, listening and noting.

We were aware of wall-to-wall regimentation and rules, such as one child per family, which everyone seemed to obey. The age for marriage was twenty-two for men and twenty for women and there were compulsory classes for happy family life and even instructions on how to be good parents-in-law. Rather awful were the choices for unmarried pregnant women – have an abortion or have the baby put into an orphanage for adoption by a childless couple.

11

Divorce and Illegitimacy

The possibility of legislation for divorce always loomed large in my mind but the perceived political wisdom was that this was a virtual impossibility. As far back as 1974 I had stated my case on the *Late Late Show* soapbox, speaking against activists Angela McNamara and Father Michael Cleary. To my mind divorce was a practical matter and all the work we had done in AIM Group and Irish Women's Aid illustrated the need for divorce legislation. After the debate I found out just how widespread and fundamental the country's opposition to divorce was, the most influential opponent of course being the Catholic Church. But here we were twelve years on and I presumed that our attitudes had shifted. I was wrong.

Realistically, summer 1986 was the last chance the ruling coalition government had to put the question of divorce to the people in a referendum in order to clear the decks before the 1987 general election. I know one government tactic was surprise: the referendum was announced without forewarning and caught the anti-divorce side unprepared. The Divorce Action Group (DAG) under whose banner most pro-divorce activists worked, appeared to have good spokespersons and be well organised. Fine Gael's campaign was organised too but not well enough. My feelings at the time were that it was badly planned and not sufficiently researched. Peter Barry was the director of the campaign and seemed to have no heart for it. Michael O'Leary, the deputy director, was, in my view, uncoordinated and a messer, and I was scarcely involved at all. There was no real opposition to the coordinated campaigns of the Catholic Church and allied groups. Women were the focus of most anti-divorce slogans and lies, which left many of them confused and uncertain. They were told that women would lose homes, children, pension rights and succession rights. Given the low percentage of women who then had jobs or independent incomes it is not surprising that they felt exposed and vulnerable. Polling day was 26 June 1986 and the result was a chastening failure – 37 per cent said yes and 63 per cent said no.

Of all the bad moments in our administration, I feel that the aftermath of the divorce referendum was one of the worst for Garret FitzGerald. He was very low and disappointed. In the past he had always tried to be positive in the face of loss, aiming to inject hope into the parliamentary party, but now he was dejected and seemed to be lacking direction. Naturally the media jumped on the question of Garret's credibility as leader. Scarcely anybody in the party fuelled the criticism, whatever views we may have held in private: to most of us in the Fine Gael parliamentary party, Garret symbolised honesty, decency and integrity. But were these qualities enough to save the party and the country from the arch-schemer Charles Haughey?

PUTTING AN END TO THE 'FILLIUS NULLIUS'

When the Status of Children Act (legislation to put an end to the concept of illegitimacy) was published at the end of May 1986, it received a positive response and great media interest. Why did it take so long, three years, to incubate? A major bill is like the iceberg, mainly underwater in the making, with very little showing on the surface. Here it was at last completed and my preference, which I secured, was to introduce it first in the Seanad. I had high hopes of a quick passage for the bill, notwithstanding the residue of bitterness from the referendum. Could we get the people who spoke so passionately about 'protecting the family' in the context of abortion and divorce to begin considering the illegitimate child as 'family'?

A government memorandum and draft bill had been published in May 1985 to give all interested parties an opportunity to comment and propose amendments. Very wide consultation followed, particularly with those who would be likely to dissent, notably the Catholic Church and the farming community. With the Department of Justice I organised their first ever public meeting in the Burlington Hotel to give people a chance to hear top lawyers analysing and debating the bill. This proved very successful indeed.

The people who worked on a daily basis on the legislation, who helped to form and amend it, were exceptional civil servants – Brian Ingoldsby, Michael McAuley and the drafter Kieran Mooney. Brian Ingoldsby, with whom I worked very closely was bright, easygoing, good-humoured and dedicated. He told me years after I had left politics that even though it seemed that the bill had taken a long time to prepare, he felt it was a quick process for such ground-breaking legislation. The reason for the lack of delay, according to him, was Andy Ward's animosity towards me. I was 'that woman' and he wanted nothing to do with me or with my work. So he was out of the consultation loop, which suited us fine.

I felt that the discrimination against and neglect of children born outside marriage was so entrenched in Irish society that the passing of the Status of Children Act should cause a spiral of change and new thinking. It would mean that all children had equal rights and would lead to more single mothers keeping their babies.

When Maura O'Dea established Cherish in 1972, a thousand young mothers contacted her for help in the first year of the organisation's existence. Most were estranged from their families; others had lost jobs; yet others had taken the old reliable solution of going to England. Cherish lobbied government and in 1973 secured payment of the unmarried mother's allowance to all single mothers. All the other issues – inheritance, property, maintenance and paternity rights – were the remit of legislation.

I felt that we should be preceded by a brass band when we took our places in the Seanad chamber for the second stage of the Status of Children Act in July 1986. This was a very high-grade Seanad: among the members were lawyers Senator Mary Robinson, Senator Catherine McGuinness, Senator Sean O'Leary, all keen debaters – as were Senators Jim Dooge, Michael D. Higgins, Bernard Durkan and Brendan Ryan. The reception of the bill was overwhelmingly positive. It was welcomed on every side. It was certainly not in the national swag bag, along with divorce, contraception, abortion and homosexuality. Media people were the only naysayers who believed it was.

This theme was taken up by Senator Brendan Ryan in his Seanad speech:

> It is worth making a point that in the past six months there has been intensive media speculation that this bill would be almost as controversial as the contraceptive legislation and the divorce referendum. They were all categorised under this utterly misleading title of social legislation and we were led to believe that there was this groundswell of opinion within the Oireachtas against reforming legislation of a social nature and this was categorised with it.

For Fianna Fáil Senator Des Hanafin, who had opposed change in the divorce referendum and supported the abortion referendum, the bill did not go far enough – he wanted labels such as 'marital' and 'non- marital' child and 'illegitimate' completely removed from the bill. He gave the legislation his total support! One concept on which all speakers agreed was that the term 'illegitimacy' would never more be used, nor any substitute like 'non-marital'. Early on I had decided to amend the bill at committee stage to reflect this.

Senator Bernard Durkan of Fine Gael took a forensic view of the Bill's provisions and made a passionate speech in its favour but it was Senator Mary Robinson who dominated the debate. She had for years been anticipating this bill and in fact had drafted a related one for the Seanad in 1974 – The Illegitimate Children (Maintenance and Succession) Bill – which had been voted out. She was at that time president of Cherish and remained in that position for seventeen years. She lobbied successfully for the organisation and was involved in many of its activities.

How did I find Mary Robinson as a parliamentary colleague? Unusual and serious. Never did an opportunity present itself for an exchange of views between us, although I shared many of hers. On days when the Seanad was sitting Mary Robinson would breeze in, head down, always carrying a heavy briefcase, climb the stairs to the chamber and deal with the business of the day. Item over, she disappeared. She wore legal black and white and no make-up. I make this point merely to indicate the change in her appearance once she had been selected as a Presidential candidate. Everything about her changed: – her hair, her make-up, her clothes – and she smiled and presented the electorate with an attractive modern young woman as a choice for President. When you add her intellectual substance, she had to be a winner!

Not for Mary Robinson the occasional visit to the members' restaurants or the bar, and she was never to be found, like others, scheming behind pillars. Everyone respected Mary Robinson and had a sense of the range of her activities on human rights issues and on behalf of the disadvantaged. I do know her legal advisory role for the early Irish Women's Liberation Movement was carried out quietly, very discreetly. She was determined to stay outside the organisation and use the law as an instrument of change for women rather than protest. On the subject of the contraceptive train she commented in her biography: 'I approved of it but I knew as a practising barrister I couldn't be part of it. I wasn't prepared to be ridiculed.'

Eventually the Seanad completed all stages of the bill and sent it to the Dáil for members to consider it and give it their imprimatur. Unfortunately this did not happen, because of the uncertainties of politics. At the time of the snap general election in early 1987, the bill was 'frozen' to await the new Dáil session. It was a bitter pill: to have to leave the almost-completed Status of Children Bill I had worked so hard on and go and fight a general election.

Lessons should be learned about legislation and the way it is processed. Most importantly, the drafting period should be better managed and a publication date given on the announcement of the legislation and adhered to. This is still not the case. I acknowledge that there can be delays when a memorandum has to be submitted to several departments for views or amendments. The file can get lost or mislaid, unless someone has an immediate role in dealing with it and forwarding it. Bills in preparation must also go to the Attorney General's office. All of this adds up to a lot of to-ing and fro-ing. Bills have to be discussed and agreed by Cabinet and all views are considered by drafters, who aim to produce a first titled copy. Even with close surveillance a bill can take years to appear. I recall children's bills and crime prevention and drink-driving measures which disappeared into never-never land but were dragged out screaming by a subsequent administration – maybe even to disappear again!

One recourse available to interested deputies is to put down parliamentary questions, asking when the legislation will be published. Standard answers are given, like next session, next year, but no detail about what is causing the delay. Another recourse is for opposition spokespersons to draft and publish their own version of the bill on the subject and have a second-stage debate. Inevitably, this version is voted out but the debate helps to focus attention on the delayed bill, gets the media interested and may even embarrass the government of the day.

THE FAMILY MEDIATION SERVICE

1986 was a busy and productive year. In April we launched a countrywide, free advice and support service for aspiring women entrepreneurs. During July I saw the realisation of the pilot scheme for family mediation. The Family Mediation Service, a free, out of court service for couples who are separating, was born. Of course the service needed money, which my department did not have, but pleading with the money ministers worked. Garret FitzGerald, understanding what I was aiming for, made sure it happened.

A steering committee I had set up in the Department of Justice identified a model that would work with our social and legal systems. A strong emphasis was placed on the children of a marriage, the aim being to have the parents discuss and agree decisions about guardianship before their separation, with the professional help of a counsellor.

Very soon the first Family Mediation centre was opened in the Irish Life Centre, its long-term administrator the very competent Maura Wall Murphy. At the end of its three-year term the pilot scheme would be independently assessed, in order for government to decide on its future. At every point I brought the best people I could find into the scheme. Tim Dalton was a fine civil servant who became involved with the mediation scheme and helped us greatly. He led a fact-finding group that visited Bristol University Family Law Department, which proved useful in our work. Tim Dalton later became Secretary-General of the Department of Justice.

Pondering on why I was able to move this scheme forward so quickly, I concluded that it was because we had the initiative. The service did not have to go to Cabinet nor through the two houses of the Oireachtas, although, of course, we had to notify other departments and take their remarks into account. But, joy of joy, we had freedom to implement a policy and it has lasted the test of time, as family mediation is now available countrywide.

Solicitor Jim O'Higgins, an expert in family law, started as chairman of the pilot group but stayed with the scheme for a number of years. At a launch dinner Jim proposed a toast to me in rhyme:

> *Finally the group reported*
> *And so mediation's started*
> *In spite of sceptics one and all*
> *It's over to our Maura Wall*
> *So, Nuala, thank you for the invitation*
> *To this super celebration*

For all your work and all your drive
In coaxing us to strive and strive
We may not always vote for you
But tonight we surely do
So lift your glasses to our host
Nuala Fennell is the toast.

WOMEN IN BUSINESS, 1986

My department had gathered some useful information by means of our report, *Agenda for Practical Action,* which the government had accepted as a blueprint for action towards equality. Our research showed that there was an extremely low take-up by women of the various state schemes awarded for starting new businesses. The figures were appalling: for instance, only 3 per cent of the IDA's (Industrial Development Authority) small industries programme and just 1 per cent of grants in the IDA's enterprise development programme went to women-owned business. Should we not find out the cause of this imbalance?

Again we tested the water, holding five conferences throughout the country. They provided information, advice and general encouragement to women interested in business. The conferences were free and more than 1,500 women attended. This showed a need for outreach programmes aimed specifically at possible women entre-preneurs.

I met Padraic White, then head of the IDA, who agreed that his organisation would designate October 1985 as 'Women in Industry Month'. They put on a great programme, which linked beautifully with what my office was doing. The result was that grants applications for feasibility studies increased by 200 per cent and 4000 women from all over the country participated in IDA events. Now we knew that business activity for women was an area of potential growth and that filling the gap would be good for the economy and for women.

Never had funds of £150,000, the amount allocated to Women in Business, been better spent. Literature, a freefone service, one-to-one free business consultancies and conferences were made available. Within a very short time, we saw results. Women tended to work in small groups or with a partner, and at the time businesses created by women included the manufacture of chocolates, mustard and a home-management company. Many other businesses were incubated at the time. It was interesting that a significant number of projects put forward for discussion in the services sector were in non-traditional areas of women's work. The services sector for women no longer automatically meant the pink-collar typing ghetto.

Everybody wanted to be part of this campaign. Even the media acknowledged its success. Much of the drive and organisation was the work of Helen Doyle, who had recently come to work in my department and had previously worked with AIM Group. The euphoria died a death once Fianna Fáil got back into government in 1987 Albert Reynolds, Minister for Industry, killed the scheme. The following day, 1 October 1987, the editorial of *The Irish Times* referred to his decision:

If the Women in Business Enterprise agency was 'patronising', as the Minister for Industry believes, then there are lot of women willing to be patronised. Within nine months of the establishment of the Women in Business Freefone advice service last year, 3000 women with business ideas had availed of it. He could have been a little more generous to the former Minister of State for Women's Affairs, Mrs Nuala Fennell, whose brainchild it was. In promoting the idea of women in business she found her role as in nothing else. She was an important force behind the IDA's establishment of its Women in Industry campaign. It is probably largely due to Nuala Fennell that next week the IDA and Aer Lingus will once again award the Women in Enterprise Scholarship to a woman entrepreneur.

Not for a moment did I consider that the Women in Business campaign patronised women – nor indeed did any of the participating women. Where one finds such a low take-up of state grants by one gender as we did, positive action is essential to enable women to catch up. It was a counter-balance to traditional thinking and ingrained discrimination. I believe that the economy of today would benefit from harnessing women's forces once again. The Women in Business campaign was certainly the right tool for women in the 1980s.

By summer of 1986 two of my important equality acts had been passed. One was the Domicile and Recognition of Foreign Divorces Act, which meant that a married woman no longer had to take the domicile of her husband who might by then be living abroad, or find herself divorced without any consultation. The second was the Irish Citizenship and Foreign Nationality Act, enabling husbands of Irish women to acquire Irish citizenship on the same terms as foreign-born wives of Irish men. I was feeling good about the Domicile and Recognition of Foreign Divorces Act and felt even better when I got a midnight call from a woman in County Mayo. She had been watching the late-night *Dáil Report* when she heard the news. She told me she danced around the room with joy and wanted to thank me, as she was a victim of the old régime.

Just when it seemed safe to come out of the water and fight another general election a new adversary appeared on the scene – a new political party, right in my own constituency, the Progressive Democrats. Mary Harney, who had been a member of Fianna Fáil for sixteen years, voted against the party in the 1985 Dáil vote on the carefully negotiated Anglo-Irish Agreement, then quit the party. Within months she had co-founded a new party, the Progressive Democrats (PDs) with former colleagues Bobby Molloy, Des O'Malley and Pierce Wyse. It spread like glue, mesmerising the middle classes with promises of lower taxation, destruction of old political moulds, high standards in public life and integrity in government. Mary Harney and Des O'Malley were the magnetic forces that drew in high-profile members, well in advance of the 1987 general election.

In my constituency of Dublin South a young PD,

Anne Colley, was establishing herself. People reported to my office on a daily basis sightings of her canvassing at all hours, 10 am on Roebuck Road, 12 noon in Stillorgan. This made my anxiety rocket. Anne Colley ticked all the boxes: she was the daughter of the late George Colley, who had been a Fianna Fáil Minister for Finance, a solicitor and pretty to boot.

December 1986 was an eventful month. On Christmas Eve the Dáil assembled to rush through the Single European Act and the associated Extradition Bill. In the High Court Judge Barrington gave an order preventing the government from ratifying the Single European Act until the constitutionality of the Act had been examined.

During that month I wrote in my journal:

> We are showing badly in the polls, at 26 per cent. The poll taken after the débâcle over the Equality legislation and the cutback in the Christmas bonus. Gemma Hussey, now Minister for Social Welfare, is going through a rotten time. Her house is collapsing around her politically speaking. She is very bitter and says she can never forgive Garret for the reshuffle mess [the Taoiseach had decided to reshuffle ministers but some of them initially refused to relinquish their portfolios.] She seems to be barely holding her own at Cabinet.

But on a personal level certain aspects of my job brought me satisfaction:

I attended the passing out parade for new
Gardaí Síochána in Templemore yesterday.
As ever it rained, even as I presented Scott
medals for bravery to two widows of Gardaí.
For me it was always a treat to have to
perform the official passing-out ceremony.
As I walked through the ranks inspecting
those wonderful young Gardaí I'd say 'Father,
see me now!'

I came back to Dublin for a date with
cabinet, with an aide mémoire for changes in
the Status of Children Bill. As I put my case
in the stuffy cabinet room, most ministers
were either snoozing or having private chats.
Paddy Cooney called them to attend and we
debated the changes needed. Garret batted
for me and the changes were passed, with
only three votes against. I found the cabinet
meeting very daunting, I suppose because I
had not been there previously, being just a
minnow minister.

Recording the Dáil adjournment vote of 19 December
I wrote:

Oliver J (Flanagan) came in for the vote and
used all his considerable dramatic skills to set
an extraordinary scene. Obviously very ill with
cancer, he had to be assisted through the lobbies
and walked with a frame. David Andrews, who
was recovering from back surgery, also came to

vote on a stretcher. The result was that a one-vote majority was announced by Tom Fitzpatrick, Ceann Comhairle. He paid tribute to Oliver, Father of the House and a true veteran of the Dáil, who was first elected in 1943. There was thunderous applause from a very full chamber and press gallery. All of which Oliver loved and acknowledged, standing over the assembled Dáil with arms outstretched, as if he were about to bless us all. It was a fitting farewell and we did not see Oliver in the chamber again. He died the following spring.

12

Bouncing Back

We made all the usual preparations for our 1987 campaign. It was to be longer than usual, four weeks. Polling day was 17 February. It was a tough four weeks. At hall doors we met with disapproval, even hostility from voters, not to me personally but to us politicians. People were angry and frightened about the state of the economy. (I imagine a situation not unlike the European and local elections of 2009.) Fine Gael's highest rating prior to the election was 30 per cent, with Fianna Fáil at 48 per cent. We knew that it was an impossible objective to hold three seats for our party in Dublin South, with the Progressive Democrats presenting a squeaky-clean image and apparently having all the answers.

On election day there were massive Fine Gael losses. Nineteen deputies lost seats, including two junior ministers, Paddy O'Toole and myself. Although I suspected I would be the one to lose out, the sense of grief was awful. I could not cry, I felt numb all over, wondering if I could have run a better campaign and feeling I had let people down: my wonderful group of canvassers, my sister Bernie, Brian and the children, my women friends who had worked so hard all month. My great and deeply committed friend Barry Coonan had been my director of elections and attempted to console me, saying I could win my seat back. But all I wanted was to go home, talk to the children and take our dogs Susie and Kim for a walk. I commiserated with some party colleagues and congratulated others.

No matter how you feel, how weary your bones are, you cannot indulge yourself. The game of politics is as much about losing as winning. A week after the election I got a morale boost. Two Fine Gael senators had won seats in Dáil Éireann and Garret FitzGerald set about replacing them until the new senate was elected. Would I accept a nomination for the Seanad seat now, he asked, and then run the six-week campaign to secure the seat? I said yes but afterwards had doubts about the whole thing. Did I have the stamina for it? What about my relationship with Fine Gael county councillors who were the major part of the electorate? This would be a tribal battle, strictly party. What if I had to suffer another defeat? Brian would not hear of such a thing and once again he was my saviour. He instilled confidence in me that right then he could scarcely have been feeling himself.

First I needed drivers for the 9000 miles journey around the country. Brian decided that enough was enough and that the children needed him at home more than I did. My brother-in-law, Joe, became one of my drivers and a friend, Peg Sheehan, was the other.

My article about my campaign appeared in *The Irish Times* of 15 April 1987:

The Seanad election campaign has to be the Lough Derg [a pilgrimage island] of election campaigns – you eat very little, sleep very little and spend a fair amount of time on your knees. Except, of course, that it lasts not for a weekend but for six weeks, costs more than £1500 and clocks up a mileage of around 9000.

I set out, a first-time candidate on the Labour panel, with substantial arrears of sleep and concentration problems. My car, if not myself, was in tip-top order with two new tyres, oil change and steering check. I threw in a couple of flasks for coffee and my daughter's all-weather sleeping bag (for night breakdowns or, as I had been led to believe, a country full of damp beds).

I soon discovered that only essential eating was possible and any problems with the car, including overheating and a blow-out which landed the car upright in a snowy ploughed field, happened where there was a choice of garages.

New candidates get off to a poor start. The Seanad campaign has a very bad reputation and no one has ever told me anything good about it. Others who have done it (and some who have not) make a point of telling the most horrific tales and predict that at the end you will be mad, or at least hallucinating and disorientated from utter weariness.

Having now had the experience and survived, I agree that it needs to be changed. Any system which involves hundreds of candidates of all parties and none charging around the country at breakneck speeds to meet and canvass county councillors, senators and deputies, is outmoded, wasteful of resources and should be examined critically.

Person-to-person contact is only part of the canvass, albeit the most important. There are also letters, endorsements from supporters, canvass cards, free pens, diaries, calendars and, it is rumoured, free bottles of whiskey in some cases.

The objective of the exercise is to meet and canvass as many as possible of your own party's county councillors, who might vote for you instead of your party colleagues on the same panel.

So, very methodically, one prepares maps and itineraries. But again it goes by the board. Any scientific or coordinated plan to achieve maximum results for miles travelled tends to be abandoned very quickly for a number of reasons. Good local intelligence is best. TD and councillor Theresa Ahearn met me in Clonmel along with the tiny baby she was feeding and advised me where to call in all the surrounding counties. I travelled well on her kindness and warmth.

Most county councillors have unstructured

lives, being also farmers, publicans, auction-
eers or teachers, and they go to an awful lot
of funerals and meetings. So they are not
always at home when you call. Any route plan
has to battle against the awful signposting.
You resort to asking for directions and the
answers were often funny: 'Take the right
fork at the silage pit at the top of the town,
or do you know where the scrap heap is, he
lives a mile beyond.' I lamented for foreign
tourists behind the wheels of cars and for
ourselves.

As I said, the purpose of the campaign is
to pursue the quarry – into milking parlours,
fields, yards, marts, funerals and workplaces.
Some knowledge of animal husbandry on my
part might have improved my standing, like
knowing the difference between a hogget
and a wether and what on earth is a brush
bull? I might have known how to respond
to tales of sick animals, or what you can do
when confronted with one.

A Leitrim bachelor councillor was preoccupied with saving the life of a tiny lamb
when we called into his kitchen. The lamb
had been savaged the previous night by a wild
mink and was in shock. The kitchen was cold
because the mammy was away in Spain and
the Rayburn stove was not lit. Undaunted,
Connie, a local woman on the canvass, came
in and took over. She filled every hot water

bottle in the house and tucked them around the lamb, covered all with a rug and left it with a good chance of survival. But despite all that your man told me his Number 1 vote was already promised.

Hospitality was of the old-fashioned kind. I was fed in every home, which helped my otherwise inadequate diet. One councillor's wife actually baked four Seanad fruit cakes as soon as the election was called.

Did you have any idea how well you were doing? Absolutely not. A call and a meeting with the voter meant they ticked you off their list and told you who else on your panel had already called. But they were mostly mum about where their vote was going.

Our pace was hectic, I would like to have lingered at Ladies' View on my way to Kenmare, or to have diverted at the signpost to the Comeragh Mountains. With the help of very good bed and breakfasts (none costing more than £10), pub lunches, Yorkie chocolate bars, apples and rural hospitality, we finished the circuit and I won a Fine Gael seat on the Labour panel in the incoming Seanad.

Meeting councillors and getting a close-up view of local politics was an education. Because Garret FitzGerald had resigned the leadership of Fine Gael during the campaign and three candidates, John Bruton, Alan Dukes and

Peter Barry, had emerged to succeed him, I was quizzed endlessly on my choice. Alan emerged as the steady favourite with councillors and I was not too surprised when he was declared the winner and new leader of Fine Gael. My opinion had been that party membership would opt for either Peter Barry or John Bruton, both excellent men and politicians in the traditional mould. To be honest, I was more preoccupied with the Senate campaign than with the change in party leadership.

THE SEANAD

Once I realised that my political career was not over, just stalled, I examined the make-up of the second chamber. Almost since its inception the Seanad has been subject to criticism of varying degrees of intensity: some wanted it abolished, others wanted it reformed. I had a good feeling for the Seanad, having seen how effectively it worked on the Status of Children Bill and its non-partisan approach to legislation. I accept that the calibre of the University senators (from both TCD and NUI) I have known has been exceptional, in that they bring some special knowledge to the Seanad and are good speakers, without droning on forever. During my sojourn in the Seanad we sat in a former waiting room, rather than the elegant former ballroom, its usual chamber, which was being renovated. My two years in the Seanad were a cakewalk compared to the previous four. I signed up for a two-year night diploma course in public relations and flew through my examination.

Meanwhile, interesting things were happening in the Dáil. In 1989 a cross-party motion sought state finance and other aid for a small number of haemophiliacs who had contacted the HIV virus from infected blood products supplied by a state agency. The plight of these people was horrific: they faced reduced life expectancy with no life insurance or pension and they felt a great need for secrecy, given the taboo around AIDS in the 1980s. Charles Haughey had taken a strong stand against the motion despite the popular support it had received. On the evening in February 1989 on which the motion was voted, Charles Haughey, en route home from a trade mission to Japan, threatened to dissolve the Dáil if the vote was lost. The government did lose but because it was a private member's bill there was no obligatory general election. Sighs of relief all around.

Equally interesting were the effects of what became known as the Tallaght Strategy. At a speech to the Chamber of Commerce in Tallaght in September 1987, not too long after his election as Fine Gael leader, Alan Dukes spelt out his approach to opposition. He said Fine Gael would not oppose the Fianna Fáil government on economic policy just for the sake of opposing. The national finances were in such a dire state that the economy needed responsible handling by whoever was in power. The Minister for Finance, Ray MacSharry, appeared to be taking a serious and practical approach to the nation's finances, so the main opposition party reached some agreement with the government with regard to decisions on cutbacks. Was the Tallaght Strategy a popular move? Not among party colleagues in general (although I agreed with it) but yes, in the public mind. It prevented senseless general elections but landed scorn and derision from his own colleagues on Alan Duke's head. I think he never recovered from it but perhaps also he might have sold the strategy better to party members.

During my time as senator, I drafted a private member's bill on mental health, to amend the draconian manner in which a citizen can be forcibly put in a psychiatric hospital on the signature of a general practitioner and with the assistance of the Gardaí. On many occasions in the course of my work I met wives who had been incarcerated by husbands as a means of resolving marriage problems. My bill was not passed but provoked public debate on a matter that was quite troubling.

BACK TO THE DÁIL, 1989

I got a phone call from Alan Dukes early in 1989 to ask if I intended to run in the next general election. My constituency colleague John Kelly had notified him that he was opting out of politics and would not be a candidate. Alan needed a commitment now to let my name go forward. Did I make an instant decision? Not quite. I was now practising as a public affairs consultant in an office quite near Leinster House and enjoying the new challenge. Earlier I had turned down an editor's job in a women's magazine, so for me there was life after politics. But the lure was still there and eventually I told Alan Dukes to count me in. Polling day was 15 June 1989.

The previous month, polls had put Fianna Fáil at 50 per cent support, Fine Gael at 28 per cent and Progressive Democrats at 6 per cent. During the campaign all the opposition parties focused on the health cuts that had been imposed by the Fianna Fáil government. It was a good strategy: Fianna Fáil lost four seats, Fine Gael gained four seats, Labour gained two seats and the Progressive Democrats lost eight seats. Dublin South sprouted the first Green Party representative when Roger Garland took Anne Colley's seat. No one was more surprised than him! During the previous six months the Tánaiste, Brian Lenihan, became very ill with hepatitis. Just before the election was called he went to the Mayo Clinic in the United States for a liver transplant. His name went forward as a candidate and he was the first TD to be returned in the 1989 election. His courage was remarkable, as was his dedication to politics, but I wondered why, at the age of fifty-nine, he was returning to the cauldron of Leinster House when he had an option to retire and enjoy life?

No party had a majority this time, so we were riveted to see how Charles Haughey would respond. The choices were: another general election which would change nothing or Fianna Fáil in coalition with a smaller party. After long negotiations with arch-rival Des O'Malley, Charles Haughey entered a coalition with the Progressive Democrats and by and large things proceeded as before. Charles Haughey gave cabinet positions to two Progressive Democrats, Bobby Molloy and Des O'Malley, and a junior ministry to Mary Harney. It was the coup to beat all coups – Mr Haughey was against the wall and the PDs took full advantage of him. Everyone was relieved when the votes were counted and we got a government. No one in Fianna Fáil took seriously the suggestion that Charles Haughey should get off the stage.

Alan Dukes and the Fine Gael front bench got ready for 'proper opposition' after upholding the Tallaght strategy for two years. Changes were happening in Fine Gael: Austin Currie of the SDLP in Northern Ireland was elected a TD; John Cushnahan, also from Northern Ireland, was elected for the party for the European Parliament; and happily my friend Mary Banotti was also re-elected to the European Parliament.

On the home front we lost our best friend: Susie, our thirteen-year-old mongrel Szitzu died. All who knew her were devastated but no one more so than my younger daughter Amanda. From the age of four she and Susie had played and romped together: Susie gave hours of joy and love and was irreplaceable. The trouble was that Amanda was in Hyannis in the US for a month, working in a candle factory on a student visa. How could we tell her the sad news? It was too stark to do it by phone or letter, so, as Amanda's sister Jackie would be seeing Amanda later in the month, she was authorised to deliver the news as kindly and gently as possible. No matter: we had several weepy phone calls in the following few weeks.

In the new Dáil I had to refamiliarise myself with the routine of a TD, a position I'd not been in since 1982. Alan Dukes gave me the job of junior health spokesperson. Ivan Yates was the main spokesperson, so I played second-fiddle to him. Ivan was a very bright young (aged thirty) politician. He could be off-putting as he was totally ambitious and self-driven but he had buckets of confidence, was brilliant with a brief, good-humoured and popular. I also became a committee member to steer a new children's bill.

By November 1990 Fine Gael had yet another leader.

Out went Alan Dukes and in came John Bruton the following Tuesday, unopposed.

It was a remarkable six months. In South Africa Nelson Mandela was freed from prison and came to Ireland, where he addressed the Dáil. My friend Ginnie Kennerley was among a small group of women ordained a priest in the Church of Ireland. How long, I wondered, would it take the Catholic Church to see women as worthy participants in our priesthood?

Probably the most spectacular event of that time was the crash of the mighty Soviet bloc. With minimum ceremony and bloodshed and with a great deal of jubilation, down came the Berlin Wall and kinsfolk were reunited in Germany. I was fortunate to be delegated by Fine Gael to liaise with our sister party the Christian Democrats in East Berlin, to help them to prepare for their first democratic general election campaign. Checkpoint Charlie was still functioning but we were equipped to deal with the bureaucracy. I could see the people were very, very poor, and the communities were flat and lifeless (as compared to West Berlin). The welcome the politicians gave our group was amazing, and their keenness to learn gratifying. A few simple concepts we take for granted they found very difficult, for instance having views on an issue, writing them down and delivering them in a speech. All they knew was how to read reams of typed script composed by others. They were uncomfortable with their own ideas. Nor was there any precedent for the door-to-door canvassing we do here in Ireland, but once we took them out on the streets they understood the importance of communicating directly and quite enjoyed it. We retained supportive links with the group.

In the later years, we travelled with teams comprising journalists, public relations experts and election organisers, including Jean Manahan, journalist Una Claffey and my sister-in-law, journalist Anne Dempsey, to countries like Albania and Macedonia. Not only was there difficulty with languages but with ethnic issues. Two Muslim women, who had to be bussed to our seminar in Tirana, the capital of Albania, had bodyguards waiting outside the room.

Back in Dublin the Irish electorate did us all the most wonderful service by electing Mary Robinson as President. It was a jubilant, heart-stopping time in my political life. Because I was a member of the Dáil I was in the audience in Dublin Castle for her inauguration. It was the first time I wore a hat to any political event. Mary Robinson had sent me a very supportive letter when I was appointed minister of state and I reciprocated after her election. I cautioned her about the 'information memos' of civil servant: many are an attempt to strangle you, if you let them. Set an assertive course at the start, I advised, and take as much control as you can. I wished her well.

So with a woman in the Park for the next seven years, I walked away from Leinster House in 1992, well satisfied with the ways in which Ireland had changed this far.

CONCLUSION

My second and last spell in the Dáil (1989-92), which lasted for two-and-a-half years, was rather unfocused except for my constituency duties and work with the Joint Committee on Women's Rights. This committee positively influenced legislation, through research and reports. We also met without the two main players of the previous decade, Charles J. Haughey and Garret FitzGerald, being in control. I missed the special dynamic they created. These two giants of politics had dominated the political stage for most of my years in the Oireachtas. They led their parties in contrasting styles, one with a strict code of compliance, and the other through dialogue and agreement.

The question most asked of all former TDs is: did you miss politics? I did, but mostly I missed my colleagues. There are no midway exits, like there are entrances in politics. One week you are *in* but next week very definitely *out*. If you do not have a job or family support it can be very lonely, and some former politicians spend a lot of time and money trying to get back into Leinster House. My time in active politics rooted in me a keen lifetime interest in politics worldwide.

In 1976 I had bought 'a room of my own', a modest

stone cottage outside Oldcastle in County Meath with three bedrooms, no running water and no loo. It cost £1,100 and after being election TD in 1981 I never saw enough of it. During 1990, Brian and I sold the cottage and bought a derelict house in south Wexford. It cost £6,500. We renovated it and spent long weekends there with family and friends and talked politics a great deal.

Part of my emphasis in this book has been on my role in the women's movement of the 1970s and 1980s but I was only one of thousands working for the cause of equality for women. There were small groups who held town meetings to spread information and to help AIM Group and great letter-writers like Mary Forde from Glasnevin, who sent very sensible letters on women's issues to newspapers. In their hundreds, women came and listened to these meetings: serious women speaking seriously. Above all I am grateful to the thousands of isolated women, severely disadvantaged wives and mothers, who contacted us and courageously spoke out. Then there were the 'big guns' like television presenter Marian Finucane and the late writer Nuala O'Faolain whose entertaining *Countrywide* summer television series broadcast the voices of ordinary women. It was also a time of women's pages in daily newspapers and magazines like *Status*, of which Marian Finucane was editor. The Council for the Status of Women, AIM Group and WPA all published excellent newsletters for some years.

Though I was not a hundred per cent in favour of a ministry for women when I was first elected in 1981, seeing the danger of marrying high public expectations with a low budget, by 1983 I had changed my mind.

The reason was that no minister, as far as I could see, seemed to be taking ownership of women's issues. I also discovered a great deal of support for women's issues from male Fine Gael TDs and believed this should be harnessed positively. Of course there were other male TDs who berated us and could be nasty, but in time most gave up or were won over. We are now all members of the Irish Parliamentary (Former Members) Society, and at various retirement functions, three of my old adversaries apologised privately to Brian or myself for past slights.

It is worth quoting an excerpt from Garret FitzGerald's autobiography, *All in a Life*:

> I asked Nuala Fennell, one of the best-known amongst the group of mainly feminist women who had been elected in the Fine Gael interest to the Dáil in the contests of 1981-82, to undertake the coordination of women's affairs across a number of departments that handle women's rights and interests. She tackled this assignment with energy and enthusiasm, but found it frustrating, because many of the civil servants and some of the ministers upon whose areas of responsibility her coordinating function impinged were notably unwilling to allow her the freedom of action she needed. In some cases this reflected a measure of male chauvinism, but for the most part it was simply the instinctive response of ministers and departments to any attempt at coordination that impinged upon their responsibilities. All in all she had a thankless task, and she found

it particularly frustrating when some of her former colleagues in the women's movement criticised her for not doing things she would have loved to do and might have been able to do, had her efforts been better received in some key departments.

Was it a thankless job? I did not find it so but it was a lonely one. One small change in administration might have made a difference. Ministers of state – and there were fifteen of us – had no scope to meet as a group, either with the Taoiseach or with the chief whip. I recall just one such meeting in 1983, and no others were convened.

What about today's women: are they living the fulfilment of our promises? More than my dearest dreams. Very many dynamic and confident women have emerged in recent decades to take an equal place with male colleagues. When I am on a plane I still notice when I hear a women captain's voice announce our route. That is what the bad old days did to me. Now there are no locked doors or chained gates against women's choices in life: instead there are reams of Irish laws and regulations that directly safeguard women's rights and entitlements. Not only do they cover women's rights with regard to employment but with regard to marriage and the family and by definition the wellbeing of children. In time laws can become irrelevant, once people develop community consciousness and respect for one another.

Epilogue by Brian Fennell

Nuala finished writing this memoir on 23 July this year. Her health had been failing over the previous few months and she had very little energy towards the end. Five years earlier she had been diagnosed with a blood disorder called myelodysplasia and we were told that her life expectancy was as little as two years. Thanks to the wonderful care and skill of her doctor, Donal McCarthy, and the nurses at St Vincent's Private Hospital, she lived for five years. Her treatment involved regular blood transfusions and her family and I will always be grateful to the many unknown people whose generosity in donating their blood gave her the precious gift of life for those extra years.

Nuala was admitted to hospital on 3 August 2009 and she died on 11 August with our children and me at her bedside.

Nuala and I met fifty-four years ago at a dance at Templeogue Tennis Club. From the instant I met her I was caught up in the whirlwind of her energy and infectious enthusiasm for life. I was totally smitten by Nuala, by the original nature of her mind and her constant refusal to accept the status quo.

In this memoir Nuala describes our time as emigrants

in Canada as well as the situation of women in Ireland in the 1960s and 1970s. I shared her campaigns on the many issues she adopted, as well as her eventual successful campaign to be elected TD.

Some of these campaigns had their lighter moments, such as the events at the male-only bathing place at Sandycove, which then displayed a notice: 'Women and dogs not admitted.' One evening during the women's campaign for equal status in the Forty-Foot, I got a phone call and the caller asked, 'Can you not control your wife?' He went on: 'Some of us men swimmers have kidney problems and can only swim at the Forty-Foot as nude bathing is the norm there, so you can't have women in.' I suggested that he and his friends find a medical solution to their problem rather than a discriminatory one. For years now females have been swimming there and the world hasn't ended.

Being a TD and especially Minister of State for Women's Affairs was a 24/7 job for Nuala. Weekends were work days as there were clinics and events in the constituency as well as meetings around the country.

Nuala's life after politics was full of activity. She started a successful public affairs business and on her own initiative organised political training courses for women in Eastern Europe, which was then emerging from the grip of communism, and in Africa. In a number of countries, including Kosovo and the Ukraine, she acted as an election observer. She was a founder of an association for former TDs and senators, of which she became the first president, and was the first woman president of the European Association of Former Parliamentarians.

Nuala loved to travel and became a fearless demon skier in her late fifties, stopping only this year because of the risks to her health. She liked to camp under canvas and every year up to last summer we spent some nights in our tent in various parts of the Continent.

Above all what mattered to her was family – her children and adored grandchildren and her brothers and sisters – and friends.

Like all couples we had our ups and downs. At times Nuala could be infuriatingly single-minded, particularly when she was in full flight on a project or cause. She was the most honest person I have ever met: she had the courage to stand up for her beliefs and fight for justice for others. She was a marvellous wife, mother, grandmother, mother-in-law and sister, and a wonderful friend to me and to many others. In her seventy-three years she touched the lives of countless people.

During Nuala's illness she never wasted a single second feeling sorry for herself. Her last words to me were: 'Didn't we have a wonderful life together?'

Didn't we just.

Brian Fennell, 20 August 2009

Appendix I

NUALA FENNELL'S LETTER OF RESIGNATION FROM THE IRISH WOMEN'S LIBERATION MOVEMENT (1971)

As one of the founder members of the Irish Women's Liberation Movement who is now resigning, it comes as no surprise to me to hear of the mass resignation from virtually all the newly formed groups in the twenty-five Dublin postal districts. For one thing it has proved that Irish women, for all the discrimination and deprivation they suffer, are not the nation of blinkered female donkeys that the small policy-making central group of women's liberationists thought them to be.

I believe and have always believed in woman as a person, free, independent and equal to a man, if this is her choice. I worked on and helped prepare the booklet *Chains or Change*, but I can no longer work for these changes with the elitist and intolerant group that is using women's liberation as a pseudo-respectable front for their own various political ends, ranging from opposition to the Forcible Entry Bill to free sedatives for neurotic elephants.

At a recent seminar it was clearly stated that if any

member, whatever her previous views, was not against the aforementioned bill, she was not in Women's Lib, and to this I can add that if you are not anti-American, anti-clergy, anti-government, anti-ICA anti-police, anti-men, then, sisters, there is no place for you either.

Perhaps this development was a foreseeable trend, the Women's Lib group in America having become a radical trouble-making anti-establishment group, while it is the National Organisation of Women (NOW) that is achieving reforms and concessions. At present I believe there is interest in such a group being formed in Dublin, that would hope to work on the national inequalities, concentrating on reform of the law, and it might be the answer for those who have been put out or off by Women's Lib.

Most members of the original founder group truly and emphatically understood the frustrations and discontent of the opting out that being a woman can mean, and were totally dedicated to group consciousness-raising and self-education, while at the same time fighting a campaign to right the wrongs. For me it is funny if not sad being discriminated against by the group for being middle-class when they are all unquestionably that, but trying hard not to show it. My last meeting, at which regional delegates attended, heard one sane voice (Mary Kenny) exhort us not to lose our identity in disproportionately fighting about the housing problem or community schools, these issues being, in fact, the bread-and-butter of other political groups – that it would be suicide for us. Her plea is too late, I'm afraid. Women's Lib has not only lost her virginity but turned into a particularly nasty harlot, and in fairness it is on this level she will be dealt with by the majority of Irish men and Irish women.

Appendix II

LETTER TO *THE IRISH TIMES* ON THE SUBJECT OF WIFE-BEATING, PUBLISHED ON FRIDAY 1 MARCH, 1974

Sir,

Can anyone who watched the TV documentary on Wednesday 27 February, *Scream Quietly or the Neighbours Will Hear*, about wife brutality in England, fail to have been chilled by the spectacle it exposed. The film was made at the Chiswick Women's Aid Centre. In England, society now acknowledges the social evil of family brutality, husbands who with almost animal aggression will beat, kick and violently abuse their wives. Mrs Pizzey, founder of Chiswick Women's Aid, can have at any one time sixty wives and more than 150 children taking refuge in her very overcrowded home. She is at least offering to women what it has never been officially acknowledged that they need: security, peace and someone who will have an understanding of what it is like to live with a brutal husband. The sentiments of some of the women speaking on the film could have come from the many letters I receive from Irish wives suffering in exactly the same way.

In the past month more than ten cases have been heard in court in the Dublin area. A quotation from one such case:

> The wife had to leave the house with two of her children. She collected the other three children from school. The children were terrified to go home, so she walked them around until evening. The husband arrived home and came into the room and struck her with his fist in the ribs. She collapsed on the floor but recovered and told her girl, aged five, to go and telephone for the Gardaí. The wife then went to a neighbour's house where she again collapsed and was then taken to hospital.

Women with this problem living in the country have solitary misery: they cannot talk about it so they write and describe the injuries they receive and their efforts to hide them from neighbours. One woman, who sent me a colour photo of her battered face, had to pretend that she walked into a post in the dark. In another case I know, the local police had twenty-five complaints of brutality made by the wife, but, because the husband is an important person in the area, they refuse to press charges. I have seen women who have had their faces cut with a carving knife, their hair pulled out in lumps from the roots, arms broken, chest and stomach kicked, in many cases incredibly, when the woman is pregnant with the husband's child.

Why do women endure this situation? Apart from

the obvious fact of financial dependence on her husband, they are tied to the home by the roles as mother and wife as well as their bond of devotion to their children. They have no money, no job and seldom the kind of contacts that will help. Women fear for their own physical survival but have even a greater concern for the emotional welfare of their children, who cannot but be witnesses to the beatings and carry the mental scars for life. Of course there is the overall need for law reform, in this area as in so many others, to give greater protection for such wives. There is also a need for psychiatric counselling and treatment for the husbands. There is a need to recognise that the women and their children should have first rights to the family home when such a crisis occurs. But the immediate need is for shelter and refuge for such women and children. None exists as of now. Wives have told me that they walked the night streets with their small children until daylight, with nowhere to rest, afraid to go home. Most cases of this kind occur on Friday and Saturday nights, but welfare agencies dealing with family problems work on a nine-to-five basis, with no emergency provisions for weekend needs.

Knowing the way the state will abdicate responsibility for any problem area in which a voluntary group is operating, I am reluctant to suggest that a home should be set up by voluntary effort along lines similar to the British one but unless the initiative is taken by ordinary people, nothing will be done.

Anyone who saw the programme and who would like more information on the situation that exists here, or who would be interested in organising a project like Women's

Aid in the UK can get in touch with the undersigned. Many Irish women and children depend on others to take the initiative to help.

Yours etc
Nuala Fennell

References

Page 77, paragraphs 3-4: *Dáil Debates Official Report*, Vol. 356, No. 2, 21 February 1985.

Page 98, paragraph 2: Hilda Tweedy, *A Link in the Chain: The Story of the Irish Housewives' Association 1942-92*, p. 65.

Page 101, paragraph 2: June Levine, *Sisters*, p. 243.

Pages 107-8: Garret FitzGerald, *All in a Life*, p. 326.

Page 119, paragraph 2: *WPA Journal*, 14 November 1979.

Page 128, paragraph 4: *Status*, October 1981, p. 27.

Page 130, paragraph 4: Garret FitzGerald, *All in a Life*, p. 397.

Page 154, paragraph 1: Gemma Hussey, *At the Cutting Edge*, p. 94.

Page 164, paragraph 3: *Seanad Éireann Official Report*, Vol. 14, 9 October 1986.

Page 166, paragraph 1 : *Mary Robinson: The Authorised Biography*, p. 68.

Pages 191-2 : Garret FitzGerald, *All in a Life*, p. 434.

Actin AIM
Informatin.
Motivation

Bibliography

Arnold, Mavis. *Irish Women into Focus*. Dublin, 1987.

Fennell Nuala. *Irish Marriage How Are You*! Dublin: Mercier Press, 1974.

FitzGerald, Garret. *All in a Life*. Dublin: Gill and Macmillan: 1991.

Friedan, Betty. *The Feminine Mystique*. New York: Dell, 1963.

Hussey, Gemma, *At the Cutting Edge*: *Cabinet Diaries, 1982-7*. Dublin: Gill and Macmillan, 1990.

O'Leary, Olivia and Helen Burke. *Mary Robinson: The Authorised Biography*. London: Hodder and Stoughton, 1998.

Levine, June. *Sisters*. Swords, County Dublin: Ward River Press: 1982.

Tweedy, Hilda. *A Link in the Chain: The Story of the Irish Housewives' Association 1942-92*. Dublin: Attic Press, 1992.

Adopt - 84

INDEX

P 83 -
Tuscale & Recognition
foreign Divorce Act 1986